BE GRATEFUL

— *Brighton College's Fallen 1939–45* —

DAVID TURNER

SHIRE PUBLICATIONS
Bloomsbury Publishing Plc
PO Box 883, Oxford, OX1 9PL, UK
1385 Broadway, 5th Floor, New York, NY 10018, USA

E-mail: shire@bloomsbury.com

www.shirebooks.co.uk

SHIRE is a trademark of Osprey Publishing Ltd

First published in Great Britain in 2019

ISBN: PB 978 1 78442 367 4; eBook 978 1 78442 366 7; ePDF 978 1 78442 365 0; XML 978 1 78442 368 1

19 20 21 22 23   10 9 8 7 6 5 4 3 2 1

Index by Zoe Ross
Layout by Myriam Bell Design, Shrewsbury, UK
Originated by PDQ Digital Media Solutions, Bungay, UK
Printed and bound by Bell & Bain Ltd., Glasgow G46 7UQ

Shire Publications supports the Woodland Trust, the UK's leading woodland conservation charity.

IMPERIAL WAR MUSEUMS COLLECTIONS
Some of the photos in this book come from the huge collections of IWM (Imperial War Museums) which cover all aspects of conflict involving Britain and the Commonwealth since the start of the twentieth century. These rich resources are available online to search, browse and buy at www.iwm.org.uk/collections. In addition to Collections Online, you can visit the Visitor Rooms where you can explore over 8 million photographs, thousands of hours of moving images, the largest sound archive of its kind in the world, thousands of diaries and letters written by people in wartime, and a huge reference library. To make an appointment, call (020) 7416 5320, or e-mail mail@iwm.org.uk
Imperial War Museums www.iwm.org.uk

FRONT COVER AND TITLE PAGE IMAGES:
Brighton College Centennial Remembrance Statue, by Philip Jackson CVO, DL, MA, FBRS. (Photographed by David McHugh)

BACK COVER IMAGE:
Joyce Heater writes in her history:

> The 12th Battalion, The Sherwood Foresters, who had made the College their headquarters before departing for France in Easter 1915, presented this brass lectern as a token of their gratitude.

(Joyce Heater, *Images of England: Brighton College*, 2007)

CONTENTS PAGE IMAGE:
Pupils working in the College archives.

Contents

Roll of Honour

Name	Cause of Death	Date of Death	Place	Age
Philip Hemsley	Killed in a plane crash	10 Oct 1939	England	23
Theodore Playford Fenn	Died when his ship was sunk	14 Oct 1939	Coast of the Shetlands	22
Peter Torkington-Leech	Killed in a plane crash	30 Oct 1939	England	26
Alexander Morton	Killed when his plane was shot down	6 Nov 1939	Germany	28
Hugh Horner	Killed in a plane crash	18 Dec 1939	Australia	27
Ian Hinton	Killed in a plane crash	26 Mar 1940	France	23
Eric McIver	Killed when his plane was shot down	14 Apr 1940	Coast of Norway	24
Dennis Jackson	Killed when his ship was sunk	26 May 1940	Coast of Norway	21
Alfred Gulley	Killed when his plane was shot down	14 Jun 1940	France	21
Leonid Ereminsky	Killed in a plane crash	17 Jun 1940	England	22
Raymond Elliott	Lost in action	19 Jun 1940	North Sea	24
Desmond Cooke	Missing, presumed killed in action when his plane was shot down	8 Jul 1940	Near Dover	33
Robert Lawrence	Killed when his ship was hit by a mine	1 Sep 1940	Dutch coast	28
Gerald Clayton	Killed when his aircraft was lost during a bombing raid	8 Sep 1940	Germany	23
Frank Stuttaford	Killed in a bombing raid	14 Sep 1940	Brighton	15
Gerald Wheeler	Killed when his plane was shot down	24 Sep 1940	French West Africa	22
Konstantine Ballas-Andersen	Killed when his plane was shot down	28 Oct 1940	North Sea	26
Philip Ripley	Killed in a plane crash	29 Oct 1940	Coast of England	27
John Oldfield	Killed in a bombing mission	6 Nov 1940	Germany	29
Henry Vale	Died in a crash while driving an ambulance	13 Nov 1940	England	46
Frank Duesbury	Killed in action	10 Dec 1940	Egypt	22
Roy Skeate	Killed in action	11 Dec 1940	Egypt	22
Harold Hobday	Killed in an accident	17 Dec 1940	Egypt	31
Donald Vine	Killed in a plane crash	29 Dec 1940	England	23
Henry Featherstone	Killed in a plane crash	1 Jan 1941	England	28
John Allen	Killed in a plane crash	1 Jan 1941	England	24

Opposite: *Detail from Brighton College Remembrance Statue, by Philip Jackson CVO, DL, MA, FBRS. (Photographed by David McHugh)*

Name	Cause of Death	Date of Death	Place	Age
Philip Gibbs	Killed when his plane was shot down	4 Jan 1941	Coast of France	21
Aernout Van Citters	Killed on active service	21 Jan 1941	Libya	32
Archibald Brankston	Died of pneumonia	29 Jan 1941	Hong Kong	31
Charles Voules	Died of wounds	17 Mar 1941	Italian Eritrea	41
Charles Piers	Killed in action	21 Mar 1941	England	21
Jack Matthews	Killed in a plane crash	26 Mar 1941	Scotland	32
Kenneth Jackson	Killed when his ship was sunk by German planes	27 Apr 1941	Greece	21
Richard Holman	Killed on active service	30 Apr 1941	England	20
Richard Fanshawe	Killed by a bomb while serving as an air raid warden	11 May 1941	England	35
James Rouse	Killed in action	18 May 1941	Greece	38
Thomas Cartwright	Killed when his ship was sunk	24 May 1941	Atlantic Ocean	25
John Humpherson	Killed in a plane crash	22 Jun 1941	England	24
Hugh Colbourne	Died on active service	26 Jun 1941	Scotland	18
George Dvorjetz	Killed in action	16 Jul 1941	Netherlands	25
Ian MacKintosh	Killed in a plane crash	24 Jul 1941	England	23
Charles Young	Killed in action	12 Aug 1941	Coast of Germany	21
Ernest Davis	Killed in a plane crash during training	14 Aug 1941	England	26
Stephen Donoghue	Died when his plane came down	15 Aug 1941	Netherlands	28
Edward Jones	Died on active service	15 Aug 1941	Middle East	27
George Watson	Killed in a plane crash	19 Aug 1941	England	20
John Bartlett	Killed in a plane crash	22 Aug 1941	England	29
Edmund Nuttall	Died of wounds	31 Aug 1941	England	40
Albert Oettle	Killed in a plane crash	30 Oct 1941	England	25
Robert Morris	Killed in action	23 Nov 1941	Libya	29
Francis Twycross -Raines	Killed in action	25 Nov 1941	Egyptian Coast	20
William Yeo	Died on active service	26 Nov 1941	Libya	24
John Paton	Died of wounds	19 Dec 1941	Malaya	22
Peter Close	Killed when his plane came down	10 Jan 1942	France	32
Ralph Stebbing	Died on active service	25 Jan 1942	Malaya	29
John Darwall	Died of disease	26 Jan 1942	Malaya	24
John Myles	Killed in action	10 Feb 1942	Singapore	22
Ian Lywood	Murdered in hospital	14 or 15 Feb 1942	Singapore	42
Laurence Sly	Died on active service	15 Feb 1942	Singapore	26
Cecil May	Killed when his ship was sunk	27 Feb 1942	Java Sea	42
Edwin Hatt	Died in a prisoner-of-war camp	1 Mar 1942	Singapore	30
Derek Jewell	Killed in a naval battle	1 Mar 1942	Java Sea	23
Reginald Nunn	Drowned after his ship was torpedoed	1 Mar 1942	Indian Ocean	49
George Whistondale	Killed in action	1 Mar 1942	Dutch East Indies	34
John Acworth	Died somewhere at sea	3 Mar 1942	Indian Ocean between Sumatra and Ceylon	44
Gerald Lonsdale	Killed in a plane crash	24 Apr 1942	Atlantic Ocean	25
George Buxton	Killed in an aircraft accident	28 Apr 1942	England	21
Michael Dawson	Died of gunshot wounds	18 May 1942	Egypt	31
Derek Normington	Missing, presumed killed, in a bombing raid	30 May 1942	Germany	22

Name	Cause of Death	Date of Death	Place	Age
David Joyce	Killed when his aircraft was shot down	2 Jun 1942	Germany	23
Hector Graham	Died on active service	6 Jun 1942	India	29
John Holdsworth	Crashed into the sea during bombing raid	7 Jun 1942	Off the Netherlands	21
Philip Groves	Killed in action	20 Jun 1942	Libya	28
Gordon Elliott	Killed in action	28 Jun 1942	Egypt	23
Alfred Fleming	Missing, presumed killed, during anti-submarine patrol	10 Jul 1942	Bay of Biscay	28
William Palmer	Killed in action	23 Jul 1942	Egypt	23
Anthony Bowes	Killed when his aircraft was shot down	24 Jul 1942	Netherlands	28
Douglas Whiteman	Killed when his aircraft was shot down	29 Jul 1942	Germany	23
Kenneth Seth-Smith	Killed in a test flight	11 Aug 1942	England	28
Brian Sargent	Killed in action	19 Aug 1942	Off France	22
Francis Mansel	Murdered by the Japanese military	27 Aug 1942	Dutch East Indies	34
Paul Crinks	Killed in action	27 Oct 1942	Egypt	26
Claud Hearn	Lost at sea	27 Oct 1942	Coast of Sierra Leone	24
Nigel Skene	Killed in action	15 Nov 1942	While at sea	35
Hubert Harrison	Died in an accident	7 Dec 1942	England	22
John Langton	Killed when his boat was sunk	18 Dec 1942	Coast of Algeria	30
Herbert Maling	Taken ill and died on active service	24 Dec 1942	Turkey	59
Douglas Lonsdale	Killed when his aircraft was shot down	3 Jan 1943	Netherlands	31
John Whitehead	Killed in a plane crash	28 Jan 1943	Australia	29
Owen Chave	Killed when his plane was shot down	14 Feb 1943	Belgium	30
Michael Allen	Died of wounds	8 Mar 1943	Tunisia	23
Alfred Sugden	Died of wounds from friendly fire	7 Apr 1943	India	40
John Peacock	Killed in action	8 Apr 1943	Tunisia	29
Cedric Thompson	Died on active service	26 Apr 1943	North Africa	27
Albert White	Died on active service	30 Apr 1943	New Guinea	36
Montagu Williams	Died on active service	29 May 1943	Wales	32
Arthur Barker	Died in an accident	5 Jun 1943	England	34
Anthony Harris	Killed in a plane crash	14 Jun 1943	USA	20
Arthur Hyams	Killed in a plane crash	25 Jun 1943	Tutuba Island, in present-day Vanuatu	31
Dennis Clark	Died as a prisoner of war	28 Jun 1943	Thailand	28
Christopher Phillips	Died on active service	12 Jul 1943	Tunisia	20
John Brydges	Died on active service	16 Jul 1943	Italy	28
Ian Wallace-Cox	Killed in a plane crash	27 Jul 1943	England	22
John Trehearn	Killed in action	30 Jul 1943	Germany	21
Derek Leader-Williams	Killed in action	6 Sep 1943	Germany	28
Peter Wray	Killed in action	17 Sep 1943	Italy	22
Martin Baxter-Phillips	Died of fever while a prisoner of war	19 Sep 1943	Burma	28
John Langton	Killed in action	23 Sep 1943	Italy	22
William Baillie	Killed when his plane was shot down	15 Oct 1943	Italy	19
Raymon Lacoste	Died on active service	20 Oct 1943	Italy	29

Name	Cause of Death	Date of Death	Place	Age
Richard England	Killed in action	22 Oct 1943	Netherlands	27
John Dixon	Killed in action	29 Oct 1943	Aegean Sea	22
John Homewood	Died on active service	29 Oct 1943	England	22
William Purves	Died on active service	18 Nov 1943	Middle East	32
Alan Toley	Killed in a plane crash	1 Dec 1943	Greece	25
Tristan Ballance	Killed in action	4 Dec 1943	Italy	27
Richard Bayldon	Killed in action	16 Dec 1943	Germany	20
Rhys Price	Killed by enemy action	5 Jan 1944	England	29
William Phillips	Died while on special operations	29 Jan 1944	Greece	26
Percy Openshaw	Died at sea	18 Feb 1944	Coast of Italy	31
Bruce Spencer	Died on active service	1 Mar 1944	Italy	28
Oscar Ackerman	Died in an aircraft collision	5 Mar 1944	Off Scotland	31
Rudolf Rouse	Killed in action	11 Mar 1944	Burma	37
Dennis Peirce	Killed in action	26 Mar 1944	Burma	25
John Stower	Shot for escaping from a prison camp	31 Mar 1944	Germany	27
Lionel Baily	Killed in a plane crash	22 May 1944	Coast of Italy	21
Gilbert Buchanan	Killed in action	22 May 1944	Italy	34
Sidney Fase	Died of wounds	4 Jun 1944	Italy	22
Raymond Belcher	Killed in action	6 Jun 1944	France	20
Joseph Holman	Lost at sea	8 Jun 1944	Off France	37
Edward Kenney	Died of wounds	8 Jun 1944	France	23
Paul Franklin	Killed in action	14 Jun 1944	France	31
William Jefferies	Died on active service	16 Jun 1944	England	31
George Russel	Died in an accident	22 Jun 1944	England	26
Gordon Fraser	Died on active service	25 Jun 1944	France	34
Robert Paine	Killed in action	8 Jul 1944	Burma	23
Eliot Welchman	Killed in action	13 Jul 1944	France	27
Patrick Ward	Killed in action	17 Jul 1944	France	27
Anthony Clinch	Killed in an air crash	21 Jul 1944	Mediterranean Sea	21
Cecil Grove	Died of wounds	29 Jul 1944	Italy	37
Lenon Tucker	Killed in action	3 Aug 1944	France	21
Paul Dawson	Died on active service	4 Aug 1944	India	36
Walter Stewart	Died on active service	5 Aug 1944	France	36
John Bigland	Killed on active service	8 Aug 1944	France	34
Gavin Galbraith	Killed in action	11 Aug 1944	France	21
Peter Moore	Killed when his plane was shot down	27 Aug 1944	Coast of Denmark	22
Günther Guhl	Killed in action	27 Aug 1944	France	24
James Hollebone	Killed in action	5 Sep 1944	Italy	31
John Fitch	Killed in action	19 Sep 1944	Netherlands	32
Roger Ward	Missing, presumed dead, on a bombing mission	23 Sep 1944	Germany	20
John Fleetwood	Died on active service	7 Oct 1944	Italy	21
Henry Thicknesse	Died of wounds	23 Oct 1944	Netherlands	44
Dimitri Galitzine	Died of wounds	26 Oct 1944	Netherlands	26
John Sulman	Killed in action	2 Nov 1944	Off Belgium	35
Charles O'Connor	Missing, presumed dead, on a training flight	13 Nov 1944	Northern Ireland	25
Alexander Pearson	Killed in a plane crash	29 Nov 1944	England	37

Name	Cause of Death	Date of Death	Place	Age
Samuel Ginn	Died on active service	3 Dec 1944	Netherlands	32
John Aldrich	Killed in action	23 Dec 1944	Italy	22
Peter Wyatt-Smith	Killed in a plane crash	5 Jan 1945	England	26
Kenneth Phillips	Killed in action	6 Jan 1945	Burma	22
Frank Holdsworth	Killed in a plane crash	10 Feb 1945	England	27
John Barder	Killed in action	14 Feb 1945	Netherlands	23
Raymond Manning	Killed in a plane crash	19 Feb 1945	Italy	21
Clifford Curtis-Willson	Died of wounds	12 Mar 1945	Germany	26
Michael James	Died following an accident while on active service	22 Mar 1945	Australia	35
Robert Scrase	Killed in action	24 Mar 1945	Germany	20
Edward Pannell	Died on active service	22 Apr 1945	Burma	25
Douglas Prince	Died soon after repatriation from POW camp	16 July 1945	England	27
Edward Young	Died on active service	24 Jul 1945	England	33
Warwick Thompson	Died of wounds	30 Jul 1945	Burma	25
Aubertin Mallaby	Killed during civil unrest	30 Oct 1945	Dutch East Indies	45
John Fellowes	Died of a disease contracted during the Western Desert campaign	8 Dec 1945	England	34
Harry Ford	Committed suicide, traumatised by experience as a Japanese prisoner of war	7 Jul 1946	England	35

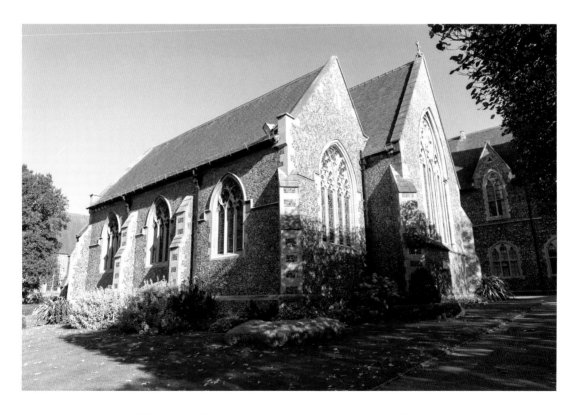

■ Above: *Brighton College Chapel from the south-east, showing the Memorial Wing.*

Sunday Express

THE PAPER THAT IS DIFFERENT

Registered at the G.P.O. as a newspaper.   JOHANNESBURG, SEPTEMBER 3, 1939.   THREEPENCE.

WAR DECLARED ON GERMANY

Britain's Ultimatum Ignored By Hitler

FRANCE WILL FIGHT TOO, CHAMBERLAIN TELLS EMPIRE

Mr. Neville Chamberlain

HIS MAJESTY THE KING

LONDON, Sunday.

THE WHOLE BRITISH EMPIRE HEARD THE DIGNIFIED ANNOUNCEMENT AT 12.15 (SOUTH AFRICAN TIME) TO-DAY BY MR. NEVILLE CHAMBERLAIN, PRIME MINISTER OF GREAT BRITAIN, THAT BRITAIN WAS AT WAR WITH GERMANY.

Mr. Chamberlain announced in the House of Commons that France had joined Great Britain in the war against Germany.

AT 12.15 (SOUTH AFRICAN TIME) MR. CHAMBERLAIN SPOKE ON THE RADIO FROM No. 10 DOWNING STREET TO THE WHOLE EMPIRE.

The British Premier's voice was steady and firm as he said: "This country is at war with Germany."

MILLIONS OF LISTENERS WERE OVERCOME WITH EMOTION AS MR. CHAMBERLAIN, IN THE MOST MOMENTOUS SPEECH EVER MADE BY A BRITISH PREMIER, SAID: "WE HAVE A CLEAR CONSCIENCE."

There was a hush throughout the British Empire as Mr. Chamberlain concluded his speech.

He said with moving sincerity in a deep voice, "God bless you all."

AN APPEAL WAS MADE TO PAY PARTICULAR ATTENTION TO THE REQUESTS MADE BY THE AUTHORITIES.

Mr. Chamberlain's Speech

Mr. Chamberlain's speech was as follows:

"I am speaking to you from the Cabinet room of 10 Downing Street. This morning the British Ambassador in Berlin handed the German Government the final Note stating that unless we heard from them by eleven o'clock that they were prepared at once to withdraw their troops from Poland, a state of war would exist between us.

"I HAVE TO TELL YOU THAT NO SUCH UNDERTAKING HAS BEEN RECEIVED AND CONSEQUENTLY THIS COUNTRY IS AT WAR WITH GERMANY. YOU CAN IMAGINE WHAT A BITTER BLOW IT IS THAT ALL MY LONG STRUGGLE TO WIN PEACE HAS FAILED.

"Yet I cannot believe that there is anything more or anything different that I could have done that would have been more successful.

Hitler would not have Peace

"Up to the very last it would have been quite possible to arrange a peaceful and honourable settlement between Germany and Poland, but Hitler would not have it.

"He had evidently made up his mind to attack Poland whatever happened and although he now says that he put forward reasonable proposals which Poland rejected, that is not a true statement.

"The proposals were never shown to the Poles nor to us, and although they were announced in a German

broadcast on Thursday night, Hitler did not wait to hear any comments on them but ordered his troops to cross the Polish frontier the next morning.

"His action shows convincingly that there is no chance of expecting that this man will ever give up his intention of using force to gain his will. He can only be stopped by force.

"We and France are to-day in fulfilment of our obligations, going to the aid of Poland so bravely resisting this wicked and unprovoked attack upon her people.

We have a clear Conscience

"We have a clear conscience. We have done all that any country could have done to establish peace. The situation, however, in which no word given by Germany's ruler could be trusted and no people nor country can feel itself safe has become intolerable.

"And now we have resolved to finish it.

"I know that you will all play your part with calmness and courage.

"At such a moment as this, the assurances of support we have received from the Empire are a source of profound encouragement to us.

"When I have finished speaking, certain detail announcements will be made on behalf of the Government. Please give these your close attention.

"THE GOVERNMENT HAVE MADE PLANS UNDER WHICH IT WILL BE POSSIBLE TO CARRY ON THE WORK OF THE NATION IN DAYS OF STRESS AND STRAIN WHICH MAY BE AHEAD OF US. THESE PLANS NEED YOUR HELP.

"You may be taking your part in the fighting services or as volunteers in one of the branches of civil defence.

"You may be engaged in work essential in the maintenance of the life of the people in time of war, in factories, transport, public utilities.

"So it is of vital importance that you should carry on with your jobs."

Right Will Prevail

"May God bless you all and may He defend the right. For it is evil that we shall be fighting again—we shall be fighting brute force, bad faith, injustice, oppression and persecution, and against them I am certain that right will prevail."

How the Premier Told the Empire

LIKE hundreds of thousands of people throughout the Empire, I choked with emotion when I heard Mr. Neville Chamberlain announce in calm and resolute tone that the British Empire was at war with Germany.

NO HISTRIONICS

There were no histrionics, no theatrical gestures from the British Prime Minister. In this most dramatic and painful moment in a long life of public service to the British Commonwealth and to humanity he was completely master of his emotions.

His announcement of the actual declaration of war—"... and consequently this country is now at war with Germany"—was clear and resonant.

But there was a catch in his voice when he spoke of the bitterness of the blow, of the failure of all his magnificent and patient efforts to preserve peace.

Hitler, "who could not keep his word," had wrecked all these efforts, but Mr. Chamberlain directed no vituperation at the man who had brought catastrophe on the world.

Never has the Prime Minister spoken more resolutely and confidently than when he blessed his listeners and declared that Britain would win.

F.B.D.

BRITISH PREMIER EXPLAINS

THE BRITISH PREMIER WAS LOUDLY CHEERED WHEN PARLIAMENT MET AT NOON. MR. CHAMBERLAIN ROSE IMMEDIATELY TO DECLARE A STATE OF WAR WITH GERMANY.

Greeted with loud cheers, Mr. Chamberlain said: When I spoke last night to the House I could not but be aware that in some parts there were doubts or bewilderment as to whether there had been hesitation or vaccilation on the part of the Government.

Consultation Held All Day

"If I had been in the same position as members, and not in possession of all the information, I might have felt the same.

"We were in consultation all day yesterday with the French Government, and we felt that intensified action which the Germans were taking against Poland allowed no delay in making our own position clear.

Official Note to Germany

Accordingly we decided to send our Ambassador in Berlin instruction which he was to hand at nine this morning to the German Foreign Secretary. They read as follows:—

"Sir,—In the communication which I had the honour to make to you on September 1, I informed you on instructions of His Majesty's Principal Secretary of State for Foreign Affairs that unless the German Government were prepared to give satisfactory assurances that the German Government would suspend all aggressive action against Poland and were prepared promptly to withdraw their forces from Polish territory, His Majesty's Government of the United Kingdom would, without hesitation, fulfil their obligations to Poland.

Preface

The Second World War began for the United Kingdom and its empire on 3 September 1939, announced over the radio to a fearful nation by a sombre Prime Minister, Neville Chamberlain. There were none of the jubilant gatherings that marked the beginning of the Great War, nor any excitable rush to enlist. There was simply a quiet resolution to get on with the job, and a sense that the British government had tried everything in its power to secure peace, but that a particularly barbarous form of nationalism had taken hold in Germany that had thwarted its every effort.

It is hard to gauge how the College community took the news, but one can imagine that the mood here too was sober. Few families had not experienced at first or second hand the brutal cost of war. The new memorial wing of the chapel stood as the starkest reminder of losses suffered, and it was here that the community gathered to hear the Head Master, Walter Hett, announce the news of hostilities.

Exactly 80 years later, the College community gathered in the same chapel to remember all those Old Brightonians and members of the Common Room who gave their lives in the subsequent six years of struggle against tyranny; this book, in large part the product of research by current pupils and their families, is today issued to every pupil in memory of their predecessors.

A number of things will strike even the most casual of readers. One striking fact is that Brighton is unusual among public schools in having lost more former pupils in the Second World War than the First. Another is that the largest number of casualties had served in the Royal Air Force (RAF) and the air forces of Britain's Dominions, reflecting the horrific casualty rates endured by RAF Bomber Command. Finally, as in the Great War, death came in many guises: the youngest victim, Frank Stuttaford, was only 15 years old when he was killed in the bombing of the Odeon cinema in Kemptown; Flying Officer John Stower was brutally executed after taking part in a mass escape from Stalag Luft III POW camp, an event immortalised in the Hollywood film *The Great Escape*; and Dennis Clark, captured at the fall of Singapore in 1942, aged 29, was worked to death by his infamously brutal Japanese captors in the construction of the 'Death Railway' between Burma and Thailand. This chapter of the war too was immortalised in film in *The Bridge on the River Kwai*.

This book encourages us to remember Frank, John, Dennis and the 170 other members of this community who sacrificed their lives in war. However, let it also serve as a reminder to us all to be vigilant in the defence of peace, particularly in these difficult days as the kind of demagoguery that plunged a world into chaos 80 years ago rears its ugly head once more.

Richard Cairns, Head Master,
Brighton College, September 2019

Opposite: Sunday Express *front page, 3 September 1939.*

Introduction

'The good die young' – or so the saying goes – and the 173 men featured in this volume, a companion to the 2016 book on the former pupils and staff of the College cut down before their time by the First World War, provides ample proof of this dictum. The 169 men educated at the school who died in the next World War and its aftermath, and the four members of staff who taught them, were a morally impressive group of men, whose very spirit of self-sacrifice steered them to brave deeds that in many cases led to their deaths. With a small number of exceptions, each one of these men was researched and documented by a particular pupil in the College's Fourth Form. I have edited down these biographies, many of them extremely well researched and some of them intensely poignant, to create a book of manageable length, while trying to fill in any gaps in information.

Though I refer to the subjects of this work as men, they should perhaps be described as men and boys – in his preface Richard Cairns has already mentioned that Frank Stuttaford was only 15 when he was killed, and the youngest Old Brightonian member of the armed forces, Sergeant Hugh Colbourne, was a month shy of his 19th birthday when he died on active service in Scotland in 1941.

There are so many acts of bravery among the 173 individuals featured in this book that it is hard to single out particular examples. Nonetheless, the seven Old Brightonians killed in the war who received the Military Cross, who carry the tag 'MC' after their name at the beginning of their entry, convey a good impression of the variety of valorous deeds, and the kind of men who performed them. The MC is awarded for 'an act or acts of exemplary gallantry during active operations against the enemy on land'; during the Second World War it was given only to officers, though nowadays it is open to all ranks. In December 1941 Lieutenant Tony Palmer received a Military Cross for organising a successful counter-attack against superior numbers. The citation lauded him for 'showing the highest qualities of leadership, coolness in action, and determination'. He was killed seven months later in the First Battle of El Alamein. Second Lieutenant Michael Allen earned the same award during the Second Battle of El Alamein, before dying five months later in Tunisia, felled by a grenade from an Italian soldier who was supposed to be surrendering. In recommending Allen, his commanding officer noted:

> During the advance he displayed great courage in the mêlées and hand-to-hand fighting which took place. Although wounded he continued to fight on, killing several of the enemy with his own bayonet and refusing to be pushed back until it was obvious that he could go on no longer.

Both these Military Cross holders were, coincidentally, the same age when they died – only 23.

Opposite: *Fourth Form pupils working on fallen Old Brightonian projects in the College archives.*

Right: *Military Cross.*

Senior officers were no less brave – as ready as the men under them to risk their lives to defeat fascism or defend their men. Two of the Old Boys in this book were brigadiers, in command of thousands of personnel. Henry Thicknesse was wounded and captured by the Germans in the Netherlands in 1944 while on a daring reconnaissance of the enemy position, and later died of his wounds. He had earlier won the Distinguished Service Order for a similar escapade in the Desert War of North Africa, during which a low-flying German fighter plane riddled the front tyres of his jeep with bullets. In October 1945 Aubertin Mallaby was shot by a teenage boy in Java while coming to the aid of one of his battalions, which had been caught up in a fight with Indonesian nationalists eager to fill the power vacuum left by the surrender of the occupying Japanese. Such men were the antithesis of the out-of-touch officer in Siegfried Sassoon's Great War poem 'The General', who smiles at the doomed soldiers on their way to the front line, while remaining tucked safely away from the action himself.

The case of Mallaby shows that it is also unfair to concentrate only on those who won medals for gallantry (though Mallaby had other decorations for distinguished service). So many men without such awards quietly put themselves in harm's way, without expecting any glory in return. One example is Flight Lieutenant Alfred Fleming, who in June 1942 was offered the safe post of aide-de-camp to the governor of Gibraltar, but turned it down to continue flying for 58 Squadron. A month later he never returned from what was scheduled to be his 50th operational mission. Twenty-one Old Boys died no less heroically in air accidents – a tally that includes both those in training and experienced pilots.

Above: *Burnt-out car of Brigadier Aubertin Mallaby.*

The worst year for Brighton College deaths was not during the dark days when the Allies appeared to be losing the war. It was instead 1944, the year when, after much hard fighting, eventual victory became certain. While those who fought in 1944 had victory in their sights, those who died much earlier in the conflict helped lay the groundwork for this future triumph. Patrick Ward won the Military Cross in 1940 during the disastrous Battle of France; he won a bar to the medal for showing equal gallantry, the day before his death in combat, during the successful campaign to win France back four years later. As a lieutenant in the 7th Royal Tank Regiment he fought desperately to delay the German advance, to allow as many of the Allied forces as possible to escape to England from the beaches at Dunkirk. Sir Basil Liddell-Hart, the military historian, later wrote:

It may well be asked whether two battalions have ever had such a tremendous effect on history as 4RTR and 7RTR achieved by their action at Arras. Their effect in saving the British Army from being cut off from its escape port provides ample justification for the view that if two well-equipped armoured divisions had been available the Battle of France might also have been saved.

These brave men, and the others featured, came from many different backgrounds. A number were the sons of professional soldiers and sailors, and some of these individuals followed their father's example by signing up for the armed services before the war as career servicemen themselves. There were also professionals with no such family background who joined up, probably out of the double motive of public service and hunger for adventure. In many cases their appetite was possibly whetted by service in the College's Officer Training Corps (OTC), the forerunner to today's Combined Cadet Force; Captain Eric McIver, killed when his plane was downed off the coast of Norway in April 1940 while attacking German shipping, enrolled in the RAF before the war, after serving as Platoon Commander in the OTC.

The lives of some of these career soldiers are fascinating. It is hard to read about Lieutenant-Colonel John Acworth without thinking that he would have made a great hero in a Rudyard Kipling story. To pay for his passage he worked as a deckhand on a boat to India, where he joined the Indian Army. In 1919 Acworth served as a squadron commander in the Third Anglo-Afghan War. He learned the local language and in Baluchistan (now in south-west Pakistan) he disguised himself as a beggar and skulked around the marketplace, where he listened to gossip and gained valuable information

▌ Above: *Flight Lieutenant Alfred Fleming.*

on the poisoning of wells and possible ambush sites for the next season's army expeditions. Men such as Acworth belonged to a world that had in some respects vanished even before the Second World War began – though a cavalry officer, Acworth tasted his first action in 1917 at Cambrai in northern France, where mounted soldiers fought alongside the new-fangled tanks that would soon utterly supplant them in the annals of war. Some of these career soldiers were the sons of professionals. Others came from civilian families, but in many of these cases, their fathers served for a time in the Great War. Patrick Ward was born while his father, Robert, was serving in a tank unit during this conflict. On his beleaguered boat back from Dunkirk in 1940, Patrick met the captain who had been in command of his father's tank company when Robert was killed in 1917.

Although Ward, and many other Old Brightonians, had chosen war as a profession, this does not mean that they were glory-seeking egotists – vain, blustering peacocks like the 19th-century US cavalryman George Armstrong Custer. As a man who won the MC twice, Ward is one of the most highly decorated of all the Old Boys in this book. However, he remained a modest man. According to his *Times* obituary:

> The French peasants still keep flowers on his grave. It is the sort of gesture he would have depreciated for himself.

At least one Old Brightonian, Johnnie Bowes, a well-liked teacher at the College for a year in the 1930s, was extremely reluctant to fight at all, perhaps because of his deep Christian faith. An organ-playing classical scholar, birdwatcher and above all entomologist – a newly discovered moth, *Oidematophorus bowesi Whalley*, was named in his honour 18 years after his 1942 death on a bombing mission – Bowes showed pacifist convictions before joining up. For example, while an undergraduate at Christ Church, Oxford, he is believed to have supported the famous 1933 Oxford Union motion, 'This House will in no circumstances fight for its King and Country', whose endorsement by the young elite of Britain scandalised the British establishment. However, when he entered the RAF in the summer of 1940, it was, as he put it in a letter, 'to help put an end to this war as soon as may be'.

It is reasonable to assume that one may know a man by his hobbies – at least up to a point. Nature-lovers are doubtless less likely to be bloodthirsty killers of their fellow men (even if, for much of the 20th century, they would have thought nothing of killing specimens). By this reasoning, Group Captain George Whistondale hardly seems to have been an excessively bellicose man. The senior officer died in March 1942 when his airfield in the Dutch East Indies was overrun by the Japanese. While heading to his office, reportedly to retrieve his stamp collection, Whistondale's car was ambushed; he and his passenger were killed.

I hope I have conveyed a sense of the variety of men and boys portrayed in this book, which broadly follows the format of the Great War volume by setting out a standardised set of facts for each entry, while also trying to create a narrative of each Old Brightonian. Where possible, the book lists place and date of birth, mother (including maiden name) and father, school and military career,

Above: *John Acworth disguised as a beggar.* ▊

place and cause of death and location of burial or, in the many cases where the body was lost at sea or elsewhere, location of commemoration. Many Old Boys married and some had children, and where we have this information we list it. However, many were too young to have married before the war, and too seldom back in Britain during it, to establish a family life; the majority of the men in this book perished without leaving a widow or children of their own. In some of these cases there may be no family left to mourn them, which makes this book all the more important.

For those men who did enjoy an adult civilian life before the war, this aspect of their existence remains often the most obscure, even though it was usually lived within these shores. This is partly because, for this group of Old Boys, the College does not have a follow-up volume to the admirably thorough *Brighton College Register 1847–1922*, which lists the career histories of Old Brightonians. It is also partly because the records on wartime life kept by Britain's armed forces are so helpful. However, in many cases we do not know for sure how men died on active service, but can surmise what they were doing and where they were by cross-checking the date of their death against the name or number of their unit. In some cases pupils have done an excellent job of finding present-day descendants, and the high standard of many of the very best pupil projects is due in part to the efforts of surviving family.

I have also tried to highlight where boys were thrown together either by College life or by the demands of war. Having overlapped at the school by one year, Flying Officer Henry Featherstone and Pilot Officer John Allen flew for the same squadron and even died next to each other when their aircraft crashed in an accident in England on the first day of 1941.

Although the vast bulk of College pupils of the early 20th century came from within Britain, a fair number hailed from much further afield. Three men in this book were born to parents of British descent living in Argentina, and one, Ernest Davis, came from Peru. His return to serve in the RAF before his death in a plane crash in England in August 1941 is all the more moving because, as a citizen of the South American country, he was under no obligation to fight. Moreover, by descent

Above: *Officer Training Corps Ashburton Shield shooting team, 1932.*

Davis was actually more German than British, and his wife, Helga, was a Peruvian of German ancestry. Why, then, did he choose to fight, and to fight on the Allied rather than the Axis side? His love for his old school, imparted in a letter to the bursar by his mother after his death, may have had something to do with it.

Perhaps the most interesting entry of all is the one Old Boy who did actually fight for the other side: Captain Günther Guhl, who had lived in Hove while his father worked as an expat, and died fighting in France in 1944. To anyone who claims that any remembrance of the dead of previous wars must invariably be jingoistic and xenophobic, please read Guhl's tale. His status as a fallen Old Brightonian was discovered by the Head of History, Martin Jones, in 1997. Considering the sensitive question of whether to include Guhl on the official roll of honour of war dead in the College Chapel, the school contacted 32 Old Boys who had served in the war. All 32 were in favour and four even asked for his brother Wolfgang's address in order to meet him.

'I lost my first husband in the last "Great War to end Wars", or so we were told. What will happen to the young laddies of 4 & 5, in another 20 years? One cannot fail to be bitter and wonder why', wrote the mother of one of the youngest of all the Old Brightonians to die in the war – 20-year-old Pilot Officer Richard Holman, killed on active service in England in 1941 – in a letter to the Head Master.

However, there was not another World War 20 years later, and even to this day Europe has seen no conflict large enough to engulf the continent as a whole, though there have been localised wars. There are many reasons for this, including a negative cause, the birth of the nuclear age; and a positive one, the germination of the European Economic Community and eventually the European Union from initial cooperation over coal and steel a mere seven years after the war's end. Another positive reason is the absence of abiding hatred against the Germans and Italians in the minds of former serving men from Britain, its Dominions, and the US, thanks to the relatively civilised nature of the war between these powers. The war in Western Europe and the Atlantic was rendered less savage by cultural ties (one exception was Flying Officer John Stower, who was executed for his role in what became known as the 'Great Escape'). When the crew of HMS *Walker* sank the U-boat commanded by Otto Kretschmer, the legendary submarine commander, Kretschmer had enough English, after a bout studying the language in the West Country before the war, to tap out 'We are sunking [sic]' in Morse code, and the *Walker* scoured the waters for the crew. Moreover, Lieutenant John Langton, Distinguished Service Cross with bar and Old Brightonian, gave them all whisky after they boarded to stave off pneumonia.

The 32 Old Brightonians who called for Guhl to be inscribed on the official roll of honour testify to this generosity of spirit that allowed both sides to rebuild trust in each other after the war. May this sense of international amity continue to prevail, regardless of what happens in international affairs over the coming years.

Above: *Günther Guhl's page in the Brighton College Roll of Honour.*

Opposite: *Poster for* The Great Escape, *1963 (see John Stower, page 132).*

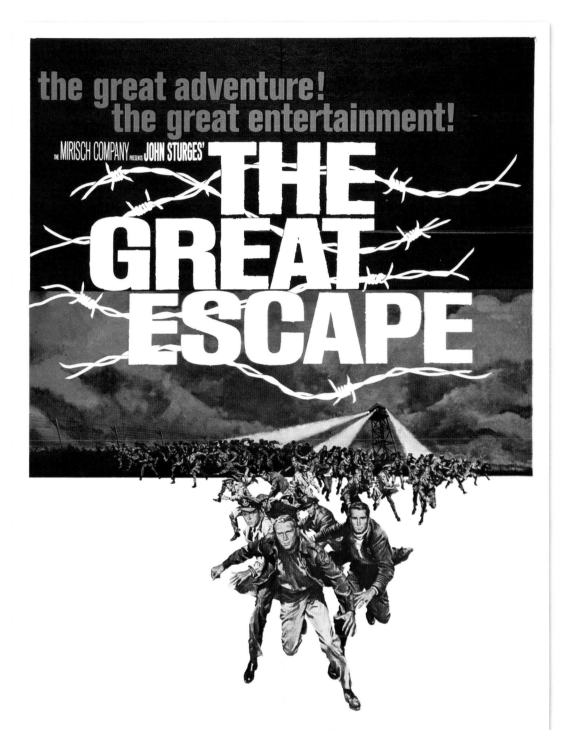

Families of the Fallen write to Walter Hett, Wartime Head Master

Walter Hett, Head Master from 1939 to 1944.

'there is little I can say on the matter – it is too sad and
there is very little left for me now.'
Julie Ereminksy, mother of Leonid (see page 36),
24 June 1940.

'It has been a very dreadful blow, but I am happy to
know he died the fine death he would have wished for,
and has left great memories behind him.'
Stella Fanshawe, sister of Richard (see page 57),
20 May 1941.

'It is difficult to realise Stuart will not come back for
the Easter holidays. His short life was a very happy one.
I cannot remember his ever having suffered the slightest
pain so he has been spared much.'
Mabel Piers, mother of Charles (see page 55),
4 April 1941.

'Knowing how happy he was there, and proud of
Brighton College, I feel it would please him very much if
his name would figure on your Roll of Honour.'
Helga Davis, wife of Ernest (see page 66),
12 October 1941.

'Thank you so much for your kind sympathy, you know
I appreciate it very deeply, the loss shakes one to greater
effort to see this madness through and get one's own back
somehow, I've lost a lot of my faith in "the other cheek"
philosophy I'm afraid.'
Charles Clayton, father of Gerald (see page 39),
19 May 1941.

'We do not know the cause of the accident, all the crew
were killed – it all seems very hush hush.'
Aunt of Ian Mackintosh (see page 65),
24 November 1941.

'You will be sorry to hear that my brother Phil – you may remember him as "Shakespeare" – has been killed on active service in the Middle East. He died from wounds in the 62nd General Corps on June 20th.'
Douglas Groves, brother of Philip (see page 89),
13 July 1942.

'Peter's death came as a great shock to us, even now I do not seem to realise it. He was a wonderful son and such a great companion. You were always so kind to him and helped him in several ways, I know he thought a great deal of you.'
Olive Close, mother of Peter (see page 76),
25 August 1942.

'Our next news was on the 12th October from Records York that he was killed in action on the 23rd September, a week after he had written his last letter. He was still a private soldier. He never liked soldiering but his letters are always cheerful and I hope to hear from someone with the 19th one day unless most of them were cut up.'
George Langton, father of John (see page 101),
October 1943.

'It has been a great shock to us all to think that these fine fellows who have done so much for us should be shot in cold blood by the Germans. One does expect to see them again when they are prisoners, they have quite enough to endure in captivity without having to end their days like this.'
Margaret Dobson, aunt of John Stower (see page 132),
3 June 1944.

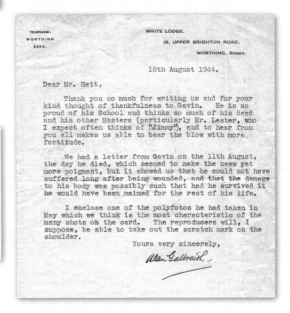

'It was such a cruel shock when my dear husband was killed, as we were both so very happy looking forward to the arrival of our baby, and it is so hard to know that he will never see him. My husband was a very fine man, and perhaps you will realize that I want his little son to know him and be very proud of him when he grows up.'
Barbara-Jean, Wife of Oscar Ackerman (see page 130), 5 June 1944.

'He had so much to come back to, and everybody loved him here as he was always so cheery and loved life so. How I pray this ghastly war will end this year.'
Marguerite Baillie, mother of William (see page 119), 15 July 1944.

'Our boy had some money saved, and my wife and I would like this to be presented to the College in memory of him. We should like your advice later as to the form the memorial should take.'
Edward Kenney, father of Edward (see page 139), 23 July 1944.

'With deepest regret we have to inform you that our only child F/Lt Douglas Weston Whiteman R.A.F. has now been officially reported killed, he has been missing since July 29th 1942, when he was pilot of a Stirling Bomber over Hamburg, he with 3 others were killed and the other 3 are prisoners of War, we have been hoping he might have escaped as we heard nothing until last month,'
William and Alice Whiteman, parents of Douglas (see page 95), 25 September 1944.

Alan Galbraith, father of Gavin (see page 148), 16 August 1944.

1939

1932 Hampden House photograph, including Philip Hemsley and Theodore Playford Fenn (see page 26).

Sergeant Pilot Philip Geoffrey Vezey Hemsley (Hampden House 1930–33)

Killed in a plane crash in England on 10 October 1939, aged 23

Philip was born in Putney, London, on 14 January 1916 to Clement Hemsley, a company secretary, and his wife Gertrude (née Johanssen). Hemsley joined the RAF at the beginning of the war and was assigned to 108 Squadron, a training unit based at Bicester in Oxfordshire. He was killed during a training flight on 10 October 1939 when his plane, a Blenheim bomber, went down. All too many inexperienced pilots died during training, but so too did many experienced ones, including, a year later almost to the day, the Czech pilot Josef František, one of the highest-scoring air aces of the Battle of Britain. Hemsley is remembered at the Runnymede Memorial to the 20,455 air force personnel who perished in the war with no known grave.

Leading Seaman Theodore Richard Playford Fenn (Hampden B House 1931–33)

Died when his ship was sunk off the coast of the Shetlands on 14 October 1939, aged 22

Theodore was born in Rangoon, Burma, on 4 September 1917. He was the son of Thomas Playford Fenn, a merchant seaman, whose own father had been an officer in the Royal Navy, and his wife Ethel (née Benskin). Given his family background, it is not surprising that Theodore went to sea himself, enlisting in the Royal Navy in 1938 and being assigned to the *Royal Oak*, a battleship.

On 14 October 1939 the ship was in the Scapa Flow naval base, in the Shetland Islands, when she was torpedoed and sunk by a U-boat commanded by Günther Prien, one of the great German submariners of the Second World War, who thereafter carried the nickname 'the Bull of Scapa Flow'. His own death while attacking a convoy less than a year and a half later – sunk by a destroyer whose second in command was fellow Old Brightonian John Christopher Langton (see page 101) – was considered so important to the Allies that it was announced in the House of Commons by Churchill.

Playford Fenn remains buried in the wreck of the *Royal Oak*, a designated War Grave.

Top: *Sergeant Pilot Philip Geoffrey Vezey Hemsley.*
Above: *Leading Seaman Theodore Richard Playford Fenn.*

Flying Officer Peter Edward Torkington-Leech (School House 1927–29)

Killed in a plane crash in England on 30 October 1939, aged 26

Peter was born on 11 August 1913 to Anne and Sidney Torkington-Leech, a South African couple living in London. During the war he served with 9 Squadron, flying a Wellington bomber as second pilot and gunner, and won temporary local fame as the first man in the squadron to claim to have shot down an enemy aircraft. He died on 30 October 1939 in a collision with another plane near Sapiston, Suffolk, and is buried at the nearby Honington All Saints Churchyard.

Top: *The battleship HMS* Royal Oak*, 1937.*

Above, left: *Flying Officer Peter Edward Torkington-Leech.*

Above, right: *Grave of Flying Officer Peter Edward Torkington-Leech, Honington (All Saints) Churchyard, Suffolk.*

Pilot Officer Alexander Donald Morton (Gordon House 1926–30)

Killed when his plane was shot down over Germany on 6 November 1939, aged 28

Alexander was born on 4 August 1911 to Edward Morton, a miner, and his wife Emily. He entered the College in 1926, winning the College cross-country race in his last year before leaving in 1930 to train as an RAF pilot.

On 6 November 1939, flying with 57 Squadron, Morton flew a Bristol Blenheim bomber on a reconnaissance mission to examine enemy dispositions on the Siegfried Line, a defensive fortification protecting Germany's border. His plane was shot down near the German town of Bad Kreuznach by a Messerschmitt Bf109 fighter plane. Morton and his two fellow crew members were killed. His remains are in the Rheinberg War Cemetery.

Flight Lieutenant Hugh Vaughan Horner RAAF (Stenning House 1928–29)

Killed in a plane crash in Australia on 18 December 1939, aged 27

Hugh was born in Melbourne, Australia, on 19 April 1912 to Eva and Harold Horner. He moved to the UK in 1928 to attend Brighton College.

In 1929 Horner returned to Australia, where he married Winifred and joined the Royal Australian Air Force Station at Point Cook, Victoria. After training at the station, he remained there as a pilot, dying during a navigational flight in an Avro Anson multi-role aircraft on 18 December 1939.

The cause of the crash was mysterious. The coroner concluded that the evidence did not enable him to say what had caused it. However, he stated: 'In my opinion there does appear to be some laxity in the manner in which the planes were serviced before flight.' Horner is buried in the Rookwood Crematorium, Sydney.

Top: *Pilot Officer Alexander Donald Morton.*

Above: *Flight Lieutenant Hugh Vaughan Horner.*

Pilot Officer Ian Percival Hinton
(School House 1930–31)

Killed in a plane crash in France on 26 March 1940, aged 23

Ian was born on 23 June 1916 in Croydon, Surrey, the son of William Hinton, a clerk, and his wife Grace (née Clark). At the College he was in the Modern Section, which concentrated on maths and science rather than the Classics. He joined the RAF in January 1939, perhaps in anticipation of conflict.

Assigned to 103 Bomber Squadron as a pilot officer flying the Fairey Battle, a light bomber, Hinton was despatched to France's Champagne region, the day before Britain declared war on Germany, as part of the RAF Advanced Air Striking Force. The conditions faced by the squadron's men show both the chaos and tensions of the war's opening months. When they arrived, the aircrews had to sleep under their aircraft until accommodation was found locally, and the initially good relations with locals deteriorated when enemy bombers started to target airfields and the surrounding areas.

On 26 March 1940 Hinton and the other two members of his crew set off for a low-level night exercise at a bombing range. Disaster struck just after take-off, when the aircraft hit a tree about two miles west of the airfield. The entire crew was killed. Hinton is buried at Terlincthun British Cemetery in France.

Top: *Avro Ansons ready for take-off.*

Above: *Pilot Officer Ian Percival Hinton.*

1940

Captain Eric Donald McIver RM
(Gordon House 1929–33)

Killed when his plane was shot down off the coast of Norway on 14 April 1940, aged 24

Eric was born on 7 December 1915 in Satara, India, to Charles McIver, a senior engineer for India's Public Works Department, and his wife Ruth (née Soldi). In 1919 mother and children moved back to England, living in Bexhill-on-Sea, though Charles continued to live and work in far-flung parts of the Empire for at least some of the time. Ten years later, McIver entered Brighton College. On leaving, he joined the military – hardly surprising, since he had been Platoon Commander in the College's Officer Training Corps. He was commissioned as a second lieutenant in the Royal Marines Flying Corps in 1934, progressing to lieutenant in 1937. In that year he began training as a pilot, qualifying in May 1938. In the summer of 1938 McIver married Diana Owen, known to all as Phyllis.

During the night of 8/9 April 1940 Germany invaded Norway. The Allies responded by attacking German ships off the coast of the country. At the time, Captain McIver was a member of 803 Squadron, based at Hatston in the Orkneys, and participated in the attack flying the Blackburn Skua, a fighter plane that also doubled as a dive-bomber, plunging from the sky to attack the enemy. He took part in the sinking of the German cruiser *Königsberg* in Bergen harbour, but in another attack in the same place four days later his plane was hit by anti-aircraft fire at a low altitude and crashed into the harbour.

Above: *Captain Eric McIver marries Diana Owen, Summer 1938.* ▮

McIver was posthumously mentioned in despatches, along with a number of comrades, two months later. This is not an award or medal but a commendation for an act of gallantry or service. All such mentions were published in the *London Gazette*. The list of names was given under the citation:

> HAZARDOUS OPERATIONS
> For daring and resource in the conduct of hazardous and successful operations by the Fleet Air Arm against the enemy, especially on the Coast of Norway.

Captain McIver is buried in the Mollendal Church Cemetery in Bergen. His son, John, was born on 9 September 1940. Having married at the age of only 22, even younger than her husband, Phyllis outlived him by 72 years, dying in 2012.

Sub-Lieutenant Dennis Hughes Jackson RN (School House 1932–36)

Killed when his ship was sunk off the coast of Norway on 26 May 1940, aged 21

Dennis was born on 14 July 1918 in Gilmerton, Scotland, to Emma and John Jackson, a major in the Royal Artillery. During his four years at the College he was a keen sportsman and athlete, winning medals in both the half mile and full mile running races.

During the Second World War Jackson served on the Royal Navy's HMS *Curlew*, an anti-aircraft cruiser. On 24 May 1940 the ship was deployed to defend Allied forces near Narvik in northern Norway, following the country's invasion by Germany. Precisely a fortnight earlier Neville Chamberlain had been compelled to resign as premier after withering criticism over the government's conduct of the Norway campaign. Two days after deployment HMS *Curlew* was attacked and sunk by German bombers. Nine sailors were lost with the ship, including Jackson.

Jackson is commemorated at the Plymouth Naval Memorial, which remembers naval personnel lost or buried at sea during the two world wars. His younger brother, Kenneth (see page 56), was also killed during the war while serving with the Royal Navy.

Above, left: *Sub-Lieutenant Dennis Hughes Jackson.*

Above, right: *Portrait of Neville Chamberlain, by Henry Lamb.*

Images of the Dunkirk Evacuation,
26 May to 4 June 1940

Left: *Soldiers wade out to a waiting destroyer (see Patrick Ward, page 143).*

Below: Dunkirk: Embarkation of Wounded, *by Edward Bawden (see Sir Edmund Nuttall, page 68).*

Opposite, top: *Still from the 2007 film* Atonement.

Opposite, bottom: The Little Ships at Dunkirk, *by Norman Wilkinson.*

Pilot Officer Alfred Richard Gulley
(Chichester House 1932–36)

Killed when his plane was shot down in France on 14 June 1940, aged 21

Alfred Richard Gulley was born on 25 August 1918, to Alfred Gulley and his wife Violet (née Scott), of Parkstone, Dorset. A bright boy, Gulley was awarded a Hampden Exhibition Scholarship on joining the College.

After leaving school he entered RAF College Cranwell, passing out in 1938 and being posted to France a few days before Britain declared war on Germany on 3 September 1939. A pilot officer in 150 Squadron flying the Fairey Battle bomber, in June 1940 he was sent with his crew on a mission to attack German-occupied roads in the Vernon Poix region of France. His plane was shot down near Aigleville and destroyed by fire when he attempted a crash landing. Gulley is buried in Aigleville Churchyard.

Flying Officer Leonid Ereminsky
(Durnford House 1932–35)

Killed in a plane crash in England on 17 June 1940, aged 22

Leonid Ereminsky (known as Ounia to his family, but Minnie, from his surname, in the RAF) was born in Russia on 29 May 1918 to White Russians: supporters of the Tsar in the 1917 revolution. We do not know what happened to his father, also called Leonid; perhaps he was killed in the turmoil and civil war following the Bolshevik takeover. At the College he was an all-round sportsman. As a boxer he had a good right hook but was 'inclined to be wild', according to the school magazine.

In 1937 Ereminsky joined RAF Fighter Command, and by the outbreak of war was a flying officer, flying the Hawker Hurricane fighter plane. He fought briefly in the skies over France before it fell to the Germans in 1940, but was soon back in England, where he joined 56 Squadron. On 17 June he led a patrol from RAF Station North Weald, but the weather quickly turned overcast. Because of this, Ereminsky decided at the end of the patrol to return at low level, but was killed when his aircraft struck the roof of a house. 'It is too sad and there is very little left for me now', his mother Julie wrote to the Head Master, Walter Hett. Ereminsky is buried in St Luke's Churchyard, Whyteleafe, in Surrey.

Top: *Pilot Officer Alfred Richard Gulley.*

Above *Flying Officer Leonid Ereminsky.*

Squadron Leader Desmond de Lancy Cooke (Chichester House 1921–25)

Missing, presumed killed in action when his plane was shot down near Dover on 8 July 1940, aged 33

Desmond Cooke was born on 28 June 1907 to Dorothy and Harry Cooke, listed at their son's death as living in Cyprus, where Harry was a civil servant. While at Brighton College he swam for the 1st VIII, and was also in the athletics team.

On 8 July 1940 his Spitfire squadron was patrolling the area around Dover, after reported sightings of Luftwaffe aircraft in the vicinity, when it was ambushed by Messerschmitt Bf109s. According to the squadron's official record:

> Squadron Leader Cooke, who was leading the patrol, took his Section through cloud, and when the rest of his Section emerged he was nowhere to be seen; attempts were made to contact him over the R/T [radio telecom], but he was neither seen nor heard of again.

It was assumed that his plane was shot down in the encounter. He is remembered at the Runnymede Memorial to air force personnel with no known grave.

■ Above: 'B' Flight of 65 Squadron, RAF Hornchurch, 1937. Desmond Cooke is fourth from left.

Sergeant Raymond Graham Elliott
(Durnford House 1929–32)

Lost in action over the North Sea on 19 June 1940, aged 24

Raymond Elliott was born on 7 August 1915, the son of a dentist, Harold, who had served in the army in the Great War, and his wife Gladys (née Way), of Steyning, near Brighton. At the College he was in the Modern Section, which concentrated on maths and science.

During the war Raymond was in 9 Squadron, based at RAF Honington in Suffolk, flying the long-range Wellington bomber. On 18 June 1940 the squadron was sent on a night mission to bomb the German town of Leverkusen on the banks of the Rhine, home to a factory owned by IG Farben, an important manufacturer of matériel for the German war effort. Unfortunately, in the early hours of the following morning, during the return flight, Elliott's Wellington was lost over the North Sea. Elliott is commemorated at the Runnymede Memorial to air force personnel with no known grave. His younger brother, Gordon (see page 89), died at El Alamein in 1942.

Sub-Lieutenant Robert Percival Lawrence RNVR
(Common Room 1937–40)

Killed when his ship was hit by a mine off the Dutch coast on 1 September 1940, aged 28

Robert was born in Nottingham on 30 November 1911 to Edward Lawrence, a bank clerk, and his wife May (née Wilde). He was educated at Nottingham High School, where he was Head of School, and then at Christ Church, Oxford, where he won a scholarship in Natural Sciences. Robert joined the staff of Brighton College in 1937, but was called up in 1940. With the typically British humour of the time, which made light of grave matters, a note in the school magazine said goodbye to Lawrence and another called-up master:

In the middle of last term, Mr. Lawrence discarded his sombre academic attire for the very imposing uniform of the R.N.V.R....We send them both our best wishes, and we are glad to know that they will both rejoin the Staff as soon as Hitler permits.

Top: *Sergeant Raymond Graham Elliott.*

Above: *Sub-Lieutenant Robert Percival Lawrence.*

Lawrence was assigned to HMS *Express*, a Royal Navy destroyer. In the summer of 1940 Britain lived in fear of German invasion, and on 31 August air reconnaissance detected a German naval force sailing towards Britain. Royal Navy ships, including HMS *Express*, were ordered to intercept, but entered an unmarked minefield, where the *Express* struck a mine. Lawrence was killed in the detonation, though the ship survived. He is buried at the Hull Northern Cemetery. An obituary in the December 1940 school magazine noted with regret:

> Sub-Lieutenant R. P. Lawrence had not been on the Staff very long, but long enough to have earned the respect and affection of all who knew him.

Sergeant Gerald Lawrence Clayton (Chichester House 1930–34)

Killed when his aircraft was lost during a bombing raid on Germany on 8 September 1940, aged 23

Gerald was born on 7 December 1916 to Charles Clayton, a wartime captain in the Royal Field Artillery who later became an architect, and his wife Olive (née Westbrook). At the College he was in the Modern Section.

In 1937 he joined the Royal Air Force Volunteer Reserve, fulfilling a boyhood dream to serve with the RAF. During the war he flew as an observer in the Blenheim bomber with 218 Squadron, which was based at RAF Oakington in Cambridgeshire.

In September 1940 he participated in a reprisal mission against Germany, which was undertaken in response to the German bombing of Britain; it was the first such reprisal mission to take place in daylight. Operating outside the cover of darkness proved dangerous: five aircraft were lost, including Clayton's. Writing to the Head Master, his father was frank about the conflict between Christian philosophy and his thoughts of revenge, writing:

> The loss strikes me to greater effort to see this madness through and get one's own back somehow. It took a lot of my faith in 'the other cheek' philosophy I'm afraid.

Clayton is commemorated at the Runnymede Memorial to air force personnel with no known grave, and at the Framfield War Memorial in East Sussex.

■ Above: *Gerald Lawrence Clayton, in the 1933 Chichester House photograph.*

Frank Peter Hugo Stuttaford (Leconfield House 1940)

Killed in a bombing raid in Brighton on 14 September 1940, aged 15

Frank was born in Brighton on 9 March 1925, to Frank Hugo Stuttaford, a GP, and his wife Winnifred (née Moore). He was a day boy at the College.

One Saturday afternoon he went to the Kemptown Odeon cinema just five minutes from Brighton College, where the Cavendish House flats on St George's Road now stand. A volunteer for the St John's Ambulance service, which rescued people from bombed buildings and took them to hospital, he decided on his own initiative to do self-imposed duty at the pictures – perhaps, like a normal healthy schoolboy, in large part because he wanted to see the double bill of films that was showing.

The second film of the double bill, *The Ghost Comes Home*, had just started when a bomb, jettisoned by a German bomber lightening its load to escape from pursuing Spitfires, landed on the cinema. This was one of four bombs from the same plane that killed 52 people in total, making 14 September 1940 Brighton's bloodiest day of the war. Passers-by and workers from the Kemptown Brewery rushed bravely into the cinema to help, beating the rescue services to it, but Frank was already dead – the youngest casualty in this book. After his death the *Brightonian* remembered him with the comment:

> He threw himself heart and soul into School life, and when the war came tried, with characteristic energy, to make himself available to his country.

He is buried in Brighton and Preston Cemetery.

Top: Frank Peter Hugo Stuttaford.

Above: Poster for the 1940 film The Ghost Comes Home.

Left: Frank Stuttaford's memorial plaque in the Brighton College Chapel.

Sub-Lieutenant Gerald Mardon Mowbray Cato Wheeler RN (Hampden House 1932–34)

Killed when his plane was shot down in French West Africa on 24 September 1940, aged 22

Gerald Wheeler was born in London on 18 January 1918 to Captain Philip Wheeler, an army officer, and his wife Constance. At the College he was in the Modern Section.

Gerald joined the Royal Air Force Reserve in 1937, and served in the war in the Fleet Air Arm, the Royal Navy's own air force. On 24 September 1940 Wheeler took part in the unsuccessful Allied attempt to capture Dakar in French West Africa from the pro-Nazi Vichy French regime. His plane was shot down by shore batteries on its approach to attack warships in the harbour, which included the almost completed *Richelieu*, one of the most advanced battleships ever built. The crew bailed out, but Wheeler did not survive. He is remembered at the Lee-on-Solent Fleet Air Arm Memorial in Hampshire.

Pilot Officer Konstantine Ballas-Andersen (Durnford House 1928–33)

Killed when his plane was shot down over the North Sea on 28 October 1940, aged 26

Born in the UK on 18 March 1914 into a globetrotting family – his father was Danish but worked for the Great Northern Telegraph Company in Japan – Konstantine captained the fencing team at the College. During the war he served with 49 Squadron of the RAF, flying the Hampden bomber. On 28 October 1940 (not November, as written in the roll of honour) Konstantine and the rest of the crew were flying home after bombing Hamburg, when their plane was shot down by a Luftwaffe fighter. Konstantine managed to land his plane within a mile of the Skegness coast, but the four-man crew perished before help could arrive. Konstantine's was the only body never found, so he is commemorated at the Runnymede Memorial to air force personnel who have no known grave.

Top: *Sub-Lieutenant Gerald Mardon Mowbray Cato Wheeler.*

Above: *Pilot Officer Konstantine Ballas-Andersen's entry in the College Roll of Honour.*

Life in Brighton takes on a wartime hue

Left: *Mrs Pitt, landlady of 'The Cricketers' Pub, pours a pint for a naval officer, 1944.*

Below: *A car passes a sandbagged barricade on the A23 near Brighton, 26 June 1940.*

Bottom, left: *Brighton beach shortly before the beach was closed and fortified in June 1940.*

Bottom, right: *Brighton seafront after fortification.*

Opposite: *Aftermath of a bombing on Bedford Street, just below the College.*

Opposite, right: *Ministry of Home Security Air Raids booklet, 1940.*

Opposite, bottom: *A map showing where the bombs fell in Brighton. Edward Batt (Hampden House 1939–44) recalls the calm wartime spirit that prevailed as the bombs dropped: 'You didn't panic, just shrugged your shoulders and got on with it.'*

Where the Bombs Fell in Brighton and Hove

This map was reproduced as a line block across six columns of the front page of the *Brighton and Hove Herald* of October 7, 1944. The *Herald* thus became the first newspaper in the country to publish a map showing where actual bombs (*not flying bombs*) had fallen on a town as reported at the time in the *Newspaper World* and elsewhere.

Official figures released at a conference at Civil Defence control on Thursday morning, October 5, were itemised as follows :—

	BRIGHTON	HOVE
Killed	1,058 plus 683 locals	1,899 including few locals
	56	27
Refugees	381	98 (including those purchase mines)
Casualties		
Seriously Injured	198	29
Slightly Injured	207	153
	413	No figures
Houses and Business Properties		
Destroyed	over 200	80
Seriously damaged	894	134
Slightly damaged	*14,232	6,792
*Including 3,500 damaged more than once		

Permission to reproduce a map came through from Regional Headquarters the following morning. The street map was obtained through Messrs. Hadlow & Sons, Ltd., Brighton (owners of the copyright), and, with the expert co-operation of the Borough Surveyor (Mr D. J. Howe) and members of his staff, the bomb "incidents" were plotted from control records. (The inset area of the street map is drawn to a smaller scale than the rest. Bombs also fell between Black Rock and Rottingdean, and on the downland behind Brighton, but are not included in this map.)

The full *Herald* issue of 25,600 copies was immediately sold out. In addition, 4,924 reprints of the map were made, and their sales realised £50 for the Sussex Maternity Hospital.

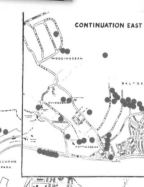

Sergeant Philip Watson Ripley
(Hampden House 1927–29)

Killed in a plane crash off the coast of England on 29 October 1940, aged 27

Philip was born in Brighton on 26 May 1913 to Georgina Ripley (née Watson), an ex-governess, and William Ripley, an insurance agent. At the College he won the form prize while in the Fourth Form. After leaving the College he worked as a bank clerk, where he met fellow clerk Audrey Outen, whom he married on 23 December 1939.

Ripley joined the RAF during the war, serving as a wireless operator with 22 Squadron, flying in the Beaufort torpedo bomber. More of these torpedo bombers were lost through air accidents and mechanical failures than as a result of enemy action, as was the case with Ripley's plane. On 29 October 1940, his aircraft crashed into the sea within seconds of take-off from RAF North Coates in Lincolnshire on a very dark night. It was thought that the pilot might have taken his eyes off the plane's instruments to check whether the formation leader had taken off. Ripley is buried in Bognor Regis Old Cemetery in West Sussex.

Top: *Sergeant Philip Watson Ripley.*

Above: *Two Bristol Beauforts of the RAF's 217 Squadron patrolling over the Cornish coast.*

Squadron Leader John Humphrey Ridding Oldfield (Chichester House 1925–29)

Killed in a bombing mission over Germany on 6 November 1940, aged 29

John Oldfield was born on 11 February 1911 in Southsea, Hampshire, to Humphrey Oldfield, a major in the Royal Marine Artillery, and his wife Emma. Oldfield was a School Prefect and member of the 2nd XV at the College, and Company Sergeant Major. He won the Prefect Prize in his final year.

We do not know what he did before the war; however, his command of an entire squadron little more than a year into it suggests he already had extensive experience of flying before war began, as either a reservist or a professional within the peacetime RAF. When war came he joined 61 Squadron, the first Bomber Command squadron to drop bombs on German soil, flying the Hampden bomber. The squadron was based at RAF Hemswell in Lincolnshire, where much of the filming of the classic 1954 war film *The Dam Busters* was shot.

Oldfield died on 6 November 1940 on a bombing mission over Germany, and is buried at Kiel War Cemetery.

Henry Charles Sillery Vale (Chichester House 1907–12)

Died in a crash while driving an ambulance in England on 13 November 1940, aged 46

Henry was British, but born in Pessac, France, on 11 August 1894. When he entered the College his father was listed as Dr C. S. Vale. Clearly a man of both bravery and conscience, he had an extremely varied life, earning his commission as an officer in the Royal Garrison Artillery in 1914 and fighting in the Great War, but then leaving the army to become a diplomat, serving in Bolivia and Chile. In 1930 he changed career yet again, resigning from the Foreign Office to enter the Church.

During the Second World War Vale volunteered as an ambulance driver for the Red Cross, and died in Catterick, Yorkshire. It is believed he was involved in a collision with a lorry. He is buried in Garforth Cemetery in Yorkshire, and left a widow, Margarita, and son, Ricardo.

Top: *John Humphrey Ridding Oldfield, in the 1926 Chichester House photograph.*

Above: *Henry Charles Sillery Vale's entry in the College Roll of Honour.*

Second Lieutenant Frank Duesbury
(School House 1931–36)

Killed in action in Egypt on 10 December 1940, aged 22

Frank Duesbury was a local boy. Born on 31 August 1918, he grew up in Burgess Hill, and was the son of Beatrice and Colonel Harry Duesbury, who retired in 1939 as commander of the Royal Leicestershire Regiment.

After leaving Brighton College, where he had been Head of School House, Frank was commissioned as a second lieutenant in his father's regiment in 1938. The following year he served in Palestine while the Arab Rebellion was in full swing.

In December 1940 his battalion was engaged in the successful assault on Italian forces at Sidi Barrani in Egypt, with Frank as a signal officer. He was fatally wounded while standing up to apply a bandage to a comrade. One of his comrades later recollected:

Frank was a fine young officer, and the excellence of the Signal Platoon, which served us so well, was greatly due to his energy and enthusiasm.

He is buried in the Halfaya Sollum War Cemetery.

Top: *Second Lieutenant Frank Duesbury.*
Above: *Men of the Leicestershire Regiment man a Bren gun near Tobruk, 10 November 1941.*

Lance Corporal Roy Carson Skeate
(Hampden House 1933–34)

Killed in action in Egypt on 11 December 1940, aged 22

Roy was born on 13 June 1918 in Plymouth to Stanley Skeate and his wife May (née Fraser). By the time he arrived at the College his mother was living in Hove. His father, by this point a retired major in the British Army, was halfway across the world in Salamaua, a staging post for gold prospectors in New Guinea that would be destroyed in heavy fighting between the Allies and Japanese in 1943.

In the war he served with the 3rd Battalion of the Coldstream Guards. He died on 11 December 1940, the day after Frank Duesbury (see opposite), almost certainly in the successful assault on the Italian defensive position at Sidi Barrani, the catalyst for the utter rout of Italian forces in North Africa. Skeate is buried in the Halfaya Sollum War Cemetery.

■ Above: *Halfaya Sollum War Cemetery, Egypt.*

Pilot Officer Harold Herbert Jordain Hobday (Chichester House 1923–26)

Killed in an accident in Egypt on 17 December 1940, aged 31

Harold Hobday was born in Clapton, London, on 19 November 1909, to William Hobday, an architect, and his wife Annie (née Paine). At the College he appeared in two Gilbert and Sullivan operettas, long the staples of public school dramatic performances: *The Sorcerer* (as one of the 'women and girls of the village' according to the school magazine) and *Ruddigore* as Mad Margaret. Archibald Brankston (see page 54), killed a month after Harold, served backstage in the same production.

Before the war he worked as a printer and married Eleanor Thorp. Their daughter, Virginia, was born in April 1940 while Harold was away on active service with 216 Squadron, flying the Bristol Bombay Mark I bomber.

On 17 December 1940 Hobday and his crew took off from the Heliopolis Cairo airfield to train at the Suez Bombing Range. Their aircraft was making a practice run over the range when it stalled and dived into the ground, killing the entire crew. Hobday is buried in Cairo War Memorial Cemetery.

Top: *Pilot Officer Harold Herbert Jordain Hobday.*

Above: *Harold Hobday (right) as Mad Margaret in the Brighton College production of* Ruddigore, *December 1925.*

Pilot Officer Donald Martin Vine
(Wilson's House 1931–35)

Killed in a plane crash in England on 29 December 1940, aged 23

Born in Eastbourne on 5 April 1917 to Sydney Vine and his wife Kathleen, Donald had a distinguished and busy time at the College, representing it in the 1st XV, Running VIII and Fives VIII, and becoming Head of House.

In December 1940 Vine was serving as a fighter pilot with 263 Squadron at Filton near Bristol, when he was assigned to escort two aircraft recently arrived from the US. The mission should have been routine and uneventful, but he flew into the ground while in cloud and was killed near Dartmoor in Devon. His remains are at the Higher Cemetery in Exeter.

Top: *1933–34 1st XV. Donald Martin Vine is on the front row, 3rd from the right.*

Above: *Pilot Officer Donald Martin Vine.*

1941

Hampden 'A' athletics team, 1935, including John Allen (see page 52), who is last on the right in the middle row.

Flying Officer Henry Edward Middleton Featherstone (Hampden House 1925–30)

Killed in a plane crash in England on 1 January 1941, aged 28

Born in Calcutta on 21 July 1912 to Edward Featherstone and his wife Catherine, known as Jennie (née Middleton), Henry was a House Prefect at the College, and played a Noble Lord in Gilbert and Sullivan's *The Mikado* alongside William Purves (see page 123).

On New Year's Day 1941 he was serving with 206 Squadron, flying maritime patrols in the Lockheed Hudson, a bomber and coastal reconnaissance aircraft. That day, his aircraft crashed into a barn wall while taking off for a transit flight at Bircham Newton in Norfolk, killing all on board. Featherstone, who is buried in the nearby St Mary's Churchyard, was accompanied in the plane by another Old Brightonian, John Allen (see below).

Pilot Officer John Buttemer Allen (School House 1929–35)

Killed in a plane crash in England on 1 January 1941, aged 24

John Allen was born on 23 April 1916 to Charles Allen and his wife Mary (née Buttemer). They lived in Kemptown, close to the College, where his father was Director of Music, and where John became Head of House. His elder brother, David, taught Maths at the College for many years. After leaving John joined the Gestetner Company, based in north London, which sold duplicating machines.

During the war he served with the RAF, and was based at RAF Bircham Newton in Norfolk. On New Year's Day 1941 his aircraft hit a barn wall and crashed while taking off for a transit flight. A fellow Old Brightonian, Henry Featherstone (see above), was on the same flight. An obituary in the school magazine noted with regret:

He was deservedly popular and his many friends will mourn the loss of an attractive personality and sterling character.

Allen is buried at Brighton Downs Cemetery.

Top: *Flying Officer Henry Edward Middleton Featherstone.*
Above: *Pilot Officer John Buttemer Allen.*

Pilot Officer Philip Evelyn Gibbs RAFVR
(Hampden House 1935–37)

Killed when his plane was shot down off the coast of France on 4 January 1941, aged 21

Philip was born on 29 July 1919, the son of William Gibbs, a schoolmaster, and his wife Evelyn. At the College he was an extremely good shot, competing for the Shooting VIII and winning an Empire Marksman 1st Class award. Had he survived the war he would probably have become a successful architect: he was awarded a distinction in his exam for the Architectural Association School of Architecture.

During the war Gibbs flew the Bristol Blenheim light bomber for 53 Squadron, which was part of Coastal Command. In January 1941 the squadron attacked enemy warships in Brest in German-occupied France. Gibbs was shot down and his body was never found. He is commemorated at the Runnymede Air Forces Memorial.

Lieutenant Aernout Schelto Van Citters
(Gordon House 1923–26)

Killed on active service in Libya on 21 January 1941, aged 32

Aernout was born in the British colony of Ceylon (now Sri Lanka) on 6 April 1908 to Aernout Henri Marie Van Citters, who was probably of Flemish ancestry, and his wife Violet (née Campbell). His father was probably a tea planter, as Aernout junior was born on a tea estate.

He presumably emigrated to Australia at some point, because during the war he served with the 2/8th Australian Battalion. In January 1941 he took part in the ultimately successful attack on the Axis fortress of Tobruk in Libya. This included a closely fought engagement where his battalion broke through the Axis lines and then repelled a counter-attack by tanks and infantry behind an artillery barrage. Citters died during this time, and is buried at the Knightsbridge War Cemetery in Libya.

Top: *Pilot Officer Philip Evelyn Gibbs.*

Above: *Lieutenant Aernout Schelto Van Citters.*

Archibald Dooley Brankston (Chichester House 1924–27)

Died of pneumonia in Hong Kong on 29 January 1941, aged 31

Born on 18 December 1909 in China, into the family of Archie Brankston, an engineer working in shipbuilding in Shanghai, Archibald was sent back to England to receive a public school education. At the College he took part in a performance of Gilbert and Sullivan's *Ruddigore* as property manager and understudy. Harold Hobday (see page 48), killed a month before Archibald, was in the same production.

A sinologist and fluent Chinese speaker, he returned to the country to work as a civil engineer from 1933 to 1935, before giving up practical for intellectual pursuits related to his country of birth. He travelled widely to study antiquities in Asia, and in 1938 became Curator in the Department of Oriental Antiquities & Ethnography at the British Museum, leaving only in 1941 to join the Ministry of Information, the wartime propaganda arm of the British government. The ministry sent him to Hong Kong on a war mission of unknown purpose. He died there of pneumonia at the age of 31.

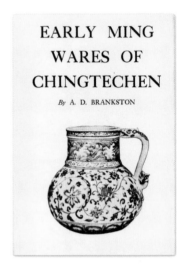

EARLY MING WARES OF CHINGTECHEN

By A. D. BRANKSTON

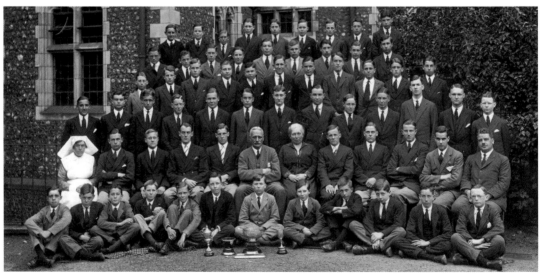

Top: *Archibald Dooley Brankston, in the 1926 Chichester House photograph.*

Above, right: *A scholarly work by the sinologist Archibald Brankston, who died in Hong Kong while working for the Ministry of Information.*

Above: *1926 Chichester House photograph. Archibald Brankston is on the fourth row, second from the left.*

Major Charles Lyon Mervyn Voules
(Durnford House 1914–18)

Died of wounds in Italian Eritrea on 17 March 1941, aged 41

Charles was born on 25 January 1900 to Mervyn Voules and his wife Julia, of Bognor, Sussex. After leaving the College, where he was Head of House, he joined the Indian Army.

In March 1941, as an acting lieutenant-colonel in command of the 3rd Battalion of the 5th Mahratta Light Infantry, he took part in the Battle of Keren, in Italian Eritrea. The Allied troops were eventually victorious in the battle, which helped eject the Italians from their colony – a rare early success for the British Army at this stage of the war. However, Voules died of wounds received in the fight, leaving a widow, Leily. He is buried in the Keren War Cemetery.

Sub-Lieutenant Charles Stuart Tristram Piers RN
(Hampden B House 1933–37)

Killed in action in England on 21 March 1941, aged 21

Charles Piers, the son of Mabel and the Reverend Samuel Octavius Piers, was born on 17 January 1920 and attended Brighton College for four years, winning the Daryngton language prize, before leaving in 1937 to join the Royal Navy as a midshipman, eventually earning promotion to sub-lieutenant. He was killed in March 1941. We do not know where his death occurred, but in correspondence with Walter Hett, Head Master of the College, his mother wrote:

All we know about his death is that he left a shelter in order to help firefighters during a terrible inferno.

He is buried in Cheltenham Cemetery, Prestbury, in Cheshire.

Top: *Major Charles Lyon Mervyn Voules.*

Above: *Sub-Lieutenant Charles Stuart Tristram Piers.*

Sergeant Jack Matthews (Hampden House 1923)

Killed in a plane crash off Scotland on 26 March 1941, aged 32

Jack was born in Brighton on 24 August 1908 to Clement Matthews, a motor engineer, and his wife Jessie (née Perrin), who was originally from Newfoundland in Canada. Jack worked as a bank clerk before the war, but this was clearly not exciting enough, and he opted to fly in his spare time. During the war he served with 612 Squadron, which conducted reconnaissance for Coastal Command.

In March 1941 he was returning to RAF Wick in a Whitley bomber after a search operation, but the plane overshot the airstrip and landed in the sea. The plane and crew were never recovered and are commemorated at the Runnymede Air Forces Memorial.

Sub-Lieutenant Kenneth Hughes Jackson RN (School House 1934–37)

Killed when his ship was sunk by German planes off Greece on 27 April 1941, aged 21

Kenneth was born on 6 March 1920 to John and Emma Jackson. At the College he played Iris, daughter of Zeus, in the Aristophanes play *The Birds*. Kenneth served with the Royal Navy in the Second World War.

In April 1941 he perished when his ship, the destroyer HMS *Wryneck*, was sunk by German planes while involved in the evacuation of troops from Greece. The Royal Navy suffered heavy losses while carrying out the evacuation, but Andrew Cunningham, commander of the Mediterranean fleet, refused to abandon the operation, famously saying:

It takes the Navy three years to build a ship. It will take three hundred years to build a new tradition. The evacuation will continue.

Jackson, who had visited the College while on leave just the month before, is commemorated at the Chatham Naval Memorial.

Top: *Sergeant Jack Matthews.*

Above: *Sub-Lieutenant Kenneth Hughes Jackson.*

Pilot Officer Richard Charles Holman
(Hampden B House 1935–37)

Killed on active service in England on 30 April 1941, aged 20

Richard was born on 23 August 1920 to Malcolm Holman and his wife Doreen of Ferring-by-Sea in Sussex. He went into the insurance industry some time after leaving the College in 1937. Richard served in the RAF during the war, flying the Bristol Beaufighter multiuse aircraft with 219 Squadron, which was tasked with protecting shipping, at RAF Tangmere in Sussex. We do not know how he died, but can surmise that his plane crashed in England, whether in an accident or because it was damaged or shot down, because he is buried in Tangmere Churchyard. After his death Richard's mother wrote to the Head Master, saying:

I lost my first husband in the last 'Great War to end Wars', or so we were told. What will happen to the young laddies of 4 & 5, in another 20 years? One cannot fail to be bitter and wonder why.

Richard Arthur Fanshawe (Hampden House 1920–25)

Killed by a bomb while serving as an air raid warden in England on 11 May 1941, aged 35

Richard was born on 18 February 1906 in Salcombe, Devon, to Arthur Fanshawe and his wife Agnes (née Tuck), but later moved to his father's original home town of Brighton, where Richard attended the College as a day pupil. He played sports at the school, but his great love was always climbing. Every holiday he would go to the mountains to climb or ski, and after leaving school he went on many expeditions, including ice climbing in the Rocky Mountains in Canada. During the war he served as a part-time air raid patrol warden in Kensington, where he lived. On the night he died he was not on duty, but, as his sister Stella wrote to the Head Master, 'when the raid got bad he went out, as he always did, to see if he could help'. He was assisting with firefighting at a big house when, according to Stella:

A high explosive bomb came down on the house and caused terrible havoc – & he was killed along with several others.

The chief warden of his station wrote to his sister praising his 'intrepid gallantry whenever there was danger' and 'his unrivalled efficiency'. Fanshawe is buried locally.

▶

Top: *Pilot Officer Richard Charles Holman.*

Above: *Richard Arthur Fanshawe.*

Above: *Poster encouraging men to join up as ARP (Air Raid Precautions) Wardens.*

Major James Edward Colleton Rouse
(Walpole House 1917–20)

Killed in action in Greece on 18 May 1941, aged 38

James Rouse was born in East Preston in Sussex on 18 August 1902 to Algernon Rouse and his wife Florence (née Rochford). He worked as a surgeon, physician and anaesthetist, and in 1929 married Nancy Murray. At the outbreak of war he joined the Royal Army Medical Corps. In 1941 he found himself in Crete when the Germans invaded. In his last letter to his wife he wrote that he thought 'I shall come through it right', but he was killed. Rouse is buried at Souda Bay War Cemetery in Crete.

Captain Thomas Desmond Cartwright RM
(Stenning and Wilson's Houses 1929–34)

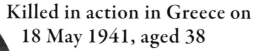

Killed when his ship was sunk in the Atlantic on 24 May 1941, aged 25

Thomas was born on 1 February 1916 in Burnham, Buckinghamshire, to Alfred Cartwright, a professional army officer, and his wife Helen (née Thompson). After leaving the College, where he was a scholar and House Prefect, Cartwright joined the Royal Marines. In August 1940 he was promoted to captain and assigned to HMS *Hood*, a battlecruiser nicknamed 'The Mighty Hood' because of her deemed invincibility.

In 1941 the *Hood* took part in the hunt for the *Bismarck*, the powerful German battleship at loose in the Atlantic Ocean preying on Allied shipping. On 24 May 1941 the British public was shocked when the *Hood* suddenly exploded while in combat with the *Bismarck*, with only three men surviving. Cartwright was not among them. He is commemorated at the Portsmouth Naval Memorial.

Top: *Major James Edward Colleton Rouse.*

Above: *Thomas Desmond Cartwright, in the 1931 Stenning House photograph.*

Ships on which Old Brightonians served

HMS Express, *a destroyer, after her bow was blown off by a mine, 1 September 1940 (see Robert Lawrence, page 38).*

HMS Avenger, *an aircraft carrier, 1942 (see Nigel Skene, page 100).*

The battlecruiser HMS Hood *with her crew paraded on deck, circa 1939 (see Thomas Cartwright, page 59).*

HMS Glengyle, *a landing craft sunk during the 19 August 1942 raid on Dieppe (see Brian Sargent, page 96).*

HMS Colsay, *a minesweeper, March 1944 (see John Sulman, page 152).*

HMS Electra, *a destroyer, with crew on parade (see John Darwall, page 77, and Cecil May, page 79).*

Flight Lieutenant John Bernard William Humpherson, DFC (Hampden House 1931–34)

Killed in a plane crash in England on 22 June 1941, aged 24

John Humpherson, son of Sidney Humpherson and his wife Lilian (née King), was born in Enfield, Middlesex, on 6 July 1916. At the College he kept busy turning his hand to various minor parts in a 1933 production of Gilbert and Sullivan's *The Gondoliers*.

Two years after leaving the College in 1934, he joined the RAF on a Short Service Commission. He had a quiet war in the months between September 1939 and May 1940, but then his air victories came thick and fast. By September 1940 he was a genuine air ace, claiming seven 'kills' of enemy aircraft, including three highly dangerous Me109 fighters, plus three of the enemy damaged, both in the Battle for France and the Battle of Britain. On 30 August 1940 he was awarded the Distinguished Flying Cross.

On 22 June 1941 a Flying Fortress belonging to 90 Squadron, with Humpherson and other crew members on board, took off from RAF West Raynham, Norfolk. The purpose of the flight was physiological research into flights at high altitude. At just above 30,000 feet, the aircraft entered a large thundercloud. The temperature in the aircraft

Top: *Distinguished Flying Cross.*

Above: *Air ace John Humpherson in the cockpit in 1941, the year he died.*

dropped by some 20 degrees, and pieces of ice began to enter through the open rear gun ports. The plane entered a steep dive, and fell apart near Catterick in Yorkshire, close to where Henry Vale (see page 45) had died in a road accident seven months earlier. None of the airmen and only one of the medical officers was able to exit the plane. Humpherson is buried in St Paul's Churchyard, Heslington, North Yorkshire.

Sergeant Pilot Hugh Anthony Colbourne (Chichester House 1936–40)

Died on active service in Scotland on 26 June 1941, aged 18

The son of Lieutenant-Colonel William Anthony Colbourne of the Indian Army and his wife Beatrice, Hugh Colbourne was born on 22 July 1922 in South Africa, but moved to England at the age of nine. After Brighton College, where he was a Prefect and member of the 1st XI, he enlisted as a pilot in the RAF, and was based at the RAF training station at Kinloss aerodrome, Scotland.

He died on 26 June 1941 in unknown circumstances, though we can surmise that his death occurred almost certainly during the course of training. He is buried at Kinloss Abbey. At a month shy of his 19th birthday, Colbourne was the youngest Old Brightonian in the armed services to die during the war, though he was three years older than Frank Stuttaford (see page 40), a civilian.

Top: *Sergeant Pilot Hugh Anthony Colbourne.*

Above: *Brighton College 1st XI, 1939. Hugh Colbourne is standing second from right.*

Sergeant Observer George Arthur Dvorjetz (Bristol House 1929–32)

Killed in action in the Netherlands on 16 July 1941, aged 25

George Dvorjetz was born in Ealing, London, on 27 March 1916 to Jacob and Rachel Dvorjetz, both originally from Poland. His father was a company director. George was a bright boy, winning an exhibition at the College, and serving as a Prefect in Bristol House. After leaving the College he became a cinema manager but also trained as a pilot, earning his aviator certificate in 1938. Joining the RAF early in the Second World War, by April 1941 he was with 21 Squadron in Norfolk.

After completing the standard number of missions over enemy territory expected of bomber personnel, he became station navigation officer, which meant that he flew combat missions only rarely. On 16 July he had the day off, so decided to go fishing in the lake in the grounds of Blickling Hall. He had just arrived when he was called back and told to report for a briefing by his wing commander, who sent him on a raid on German shipping in Rotterdam.

Dvorjetz's aircraft was hit by anti-aircraft fire over Rotterdam. According to eyewitnesses, the pilot initially tried to land in a park with a large playground, but realised that it was full of children and their mothers. He ascended again in a bid to land in a canal, but the plane's wing tip hit a building and the plane plunged into the bank of the canal, killing all occupants.

Every year local people, including the children of a nearby school, commemorate the self-sacrifice of an aircrew who appear to have greatly reduced their own chances of surviving to save innocent civilians. George's remains lie in the Crooswijk Cemetery in Rotterdam.

Top: *Sergeant Observer George Arthur Dvorjetz.*

Above: *Low-level oblique aerial photograph taken during a daylight raid on the docks at Rotterdam by Bristol Blenheim Mark IVs of No. 2 Group. Bombs burst on the docks by the Nieuwe Maas as a Blenheim banks away after its attack.*

Sergeant Pilot Ian Robert MacKintosh (Hampden House 1932–36)

Killed in a plane crash in England on 24 July 1941, aged 23

Ian MacKintosh was born in Rio de Janeiro on 18 June 1918 to Charles MacKintosh, a banker, and his wife Margaret. Ian came to England in 1928, aged nine, with his mother and siblings. At the age of 13 he joined Brighton College, becoming Head of House in his final year.

MacKintosh died on active service on 24 July 1941, while serving with the RAF. Writing to the Head Master, Ian's aunt related that her nephew was killed in an accident whilst carrying out operational night flying. She added that the cause of the accident was unknown, that the family did not know much about it, and that it all seemed 'very hush-hush'. MacKintosh's grave is in St John's Chapel Churchyard, Long Lawford, Warwickshire.

Sergeant Charles Frederick Young (Durnford House 1932–36)

Killed in action off the coast of Germany on 12 August 1941, aged 21

Charles was born on 21 September 1919, the only child of Frederick Young, an optician in Worthing, and his wife Evelyn. After four years as a day pupil in Durnford House, he volunteered for the RAF. By the beginning of the war Young was in 149 Squadron, a night bomber unit. The squadron flew the Vickers Wellington.

In August 1941 a crew including Young took off from RAF Mildenhall in Suffolk to carry out an early trial of 'GEE', a top-secret new navigation aid for bomber crews. GEE measured the time delay between two radio signals to produce a fix, with an accuracy of a few hundred metres at ranges up to about 350 miles. For large, fixed targets, such as the cities that were attacked at night, GEE offered enough accuracy to be used as an aiming reference without the need for a bombsight or other external reference.

Young's plane is believed to have been damaged over Hanover before finally coming down near Sylt, a German island in the North Sea. The bodies of the crew were never recovered, so he is commemorated at the Runnymede Air Forces Memorial.

Top: *Sergeant Pilot Ian Robert MacKintosh.*

Above: *Sergeant Charles Frederick Young.*

Pilot Officer Ernest René Davis
(Chichester House 1929–31)

Killed in a plane crash during training in England on 14 August 1941, aged 26

One of the most intriguing cases in this book is that of Ernest Davis, born on 21 July 1915 in Antofagasta, Chile, to Luz Davis (née Alexander) and Christian Davis (né Kucheler).

When war came he enlisted in the RAF, despite being a citizen of Peru and coming from a family arguably more German than British – his paternal grandfather had been born a German and his wife, Helga Braasch, was a Peruvian of German descent. One reason for his decision to fight for the Allies may have been his love of Brighton College, which he entered in 1929. He was somewhat late for term, for the fully understandable reason that it took many days to travel by boat from South America. A few months after Davis' death, his wife wrote to the bursar to inform the school about it. In her correspondence with the school, she wrote:

> Knowing how happy he was there, and proud of Brighton College, I feel it would please him very much if his name would figure in your Roll of Honour.

After going back to Peru, he returned to the UK in March 1940 and trained as a pilot officer in 83 Squadron of Bomber Command, based at RAF Scampton, Lincolnshire. It was during this training that he crashed in Worcestershire while practising night flying in his Hampden bomber. His grave can be found in the churchyard of St John the Baptist, close to his airbase.

Sergeant Observer Stephen Philip Donoghue
(School House 1927–30)

Died when his plane came down over the Netherlands on 15 August 1941, aged 28

Philip was born on 13 December 1912 in Welwyn Garden City, Hertfordshire, to Stephen Donoghue, a jockey, and his wife Bridie. At the College Philip raced on his own two feet rather than a horse's four: he was a strong cross-country runner.

During the war he flew as an observer in Armstrong Whitley bombers with 51 Squadron, based at RAF Dishforth in Yorkshire. On 15 August 1941 his plane came down over the Netherlands, either en route to or on the return journey from a bombing mission. Philip left a widow, Olwyn, and is buried at the Schiermonnikoog Cemetery.

Top: Pilot Officer Ernest René Davis.

Above: Sergeant Observer Stephen Philip Donoghue.

Driver Edward Brereton Jones (School House 1927–30)

Died on active service in the Middle East on 15 August 1941, aged 27

Edward Jones was born on 27 August 1913 in Edmonton, Middlesex, to Louisa Jones (née Ramsay) and Rev. Henry Jones, both originally from Uruguay. A physically imposing man – described as 'a very big fellow' in correspondence between an Old Boy and the College after his death – he joined School House in 1927, and after leaving the College became a land agent in Edinburgh.

During the war he served as a driver in the transport section of the Royal Army Supply Corps. We know nothing of how Jones died, despite the best efforts of the Head Master, who wrote to several officers trying to get to the bottom of the mystery. He is buried in Israel's Ramleh War Cemetery.

Leading Airman George Ronald Watson (School House 1933–38)

Killed in a plane crash in England on 19 August 1941, aged 20

George Watson was born on 8 June 1921 in Edinburgh to Elsie and James Watson. When he left the College in 1938, the reason for removal was listed as 'war', showing the mounting nervousness about conflict, particularly on the south coast, at this early stage. After school he studied aeronautical engineering in Hatfield, Hertfordshire, probably at the De Havilland Aeronautical Technical School. He enrolled in the Royal Navy in 1941, to train as a pilot at Netheravon Air Field Camp on Salisbury Plain in Wiltshire.

On 19 August, he was flying a Hawker Hart light bomber, with a fellow pilot acting as navigator. The plane flew into the ground half a mile south-east of Claverton Church, three miles east-south-east of Bath. The official records state that the pilots had decided to engage in 'unauthorised low-flying'. As a consequence, they hit electricity cables and crashed in flames. However, there were high winds on the day, which may have affected the flying conditions. In writing to the Head Master about George's death, his mother also expressed concerns about his younger brother Leslie, who was still at the school:

> Leslie had a very sad holiday, as he & Ronald were such close pals as they spent most of their lives together being educated at the same schools. I hope it doesn't affect his work & games this term.

Watson is buried in the cemetery of All Saints Church, Netheravon.

Top: *Driver Edward Brereton Jones.*

Above: *Leading Airman George Ronald Watson.*

Wing Commander John Stuart Bartlett, DFC (Stenning House 1926–32)

Killed in a plane crash in England on 22 August 1941, aged 29

John was born on the Isle of Wight on 1 August 1912 to Arthur Bartlett, a bank manager, and his wife Maud (née King). At the College he captained the athletics team, played fives, and was a stalwart of the 1st XV. He was clearly a fearless player, because the College magazine records that he suffered several injuries. This sporting grit doubtless helped in his rise to Head of School.

After College he joined the RAF on a Short Service Commission, which ended in March 1939. However, he swiftly re-enlisted when war came, flying bombers, earning the Distinguished Flying Cross, and surviving two narrow escapes: one when he was hit by flak but still managed a safe landing, and one when he ran out of fuel off Margate when returning from a mission – Bartlett and his crew rowed ashore in a dinghy.

By August 1941 he was an acting wing commander and a member of 255 Squadron at RAF Coltishall in Norfolk. That month, his Bristol Beaufighter crashed on its final approach to the airfield, killing Bartlett and a fellow crew member. He is buried at the Brookwood Military Cemetery in Surrey.

Lieutenant-Colonel Sir Edmund Keith Nuttall, Baronet (Chichester House 1915–20)

Died of wounds in England on 31 August 1941, aged 40

Edmund was born on 27 March 1901 to Sir Edmund Nuttall, 1st Baronet, and his wife Ethel (née Lillington). The Nuttalls were a rich family of industrialists, drawing wealth and prestige from a construction engineering business founded in Manchester in 1865 by an ancestor. At the College he was Head of House. Edmund junior succeeded to the baronetcy and the chairmanship on the death of his father in 1923. However, he decided not to forge a career in the engineering workshops of his company but in the military, in – where else? – the Royal Engineers. He took part in the 1940 Battle for France and was mentioned in despatches, but was severely wounded at Dunkirk, where the British forces escaped during the fall of France in 1940, and later died of his wounds. He is buried in Lowesby (All Saints) Churchyard in Leicestershire.

Top: *Wing Commander John Stuart Bartlett, DFC.*

Above: *Lieutenant-Colonel Sir Edmund Keith Nuttall, Baronet.*

Flight Lieutenant Albert John Oettle, DFC (Stenning and Hampden Houses 1930–34)

Killed in a plane crash in England on 30 October 1941, aged 25

Albert was born on 26 September 1916 in Surbiton, Surrey, to Albert Oettle, a prosperous baker and son of a naturalised German, and his wife Alice (née West). During the Great War many people of German ancestry anglicised their surnames, but his family appears to have felt secure with its original name. He played percussion in a College production of Gilbert and Sullivan's *H.M.S. Pinafore*, and returned to help in the same role the next year in *The Mikado* despite having left the school.

In 1937 he joined the RAF. During the war he flew the Whitley bomber for 51 Squadron, earning the Distinguished Flying Cross for bombing operations. In October 1941 his plane stalled on landing at the end of a routine flight within England, and crashed at RAF Stradishall in Suffolk. He is buried at St Andrew's Church, Hove.

Gunner Robert Morris (Durnford House 1926–29)

Killed in action in Libya on 23 November 1941, aged 29

Robert Morris was born on 31 January 1912 to Reginald and Vivienne Morris. After leaving the College he managed the office of a firm of estate agents, architects and surveyors in Esher, Surrey. In 1937 he married Betty Noble and they had a daughter, Jane.

When war began he joined the army immediately. Correspondence with Walter Hett shows that Robert was keen to be accepted for officer training, rather than being a member of the ranks, and wanted Hett to give him a reference. Although Hett did so, this did not seem to do the trick, and he spent his war as a gunner in the 1st Light Anti-Aircraft Regiment of the Royal Artillery. In May 1941 the regiment was posted to North Africa. Gunner Morris died on 23 November defending the Sidi Rezegh Airfield against the Germans. He is buried at the Knightsbridge War Cemetery in Libya.

Top: *Flight Lieutenant Albert John Oettle, DFC.*

Above: *A Bofors anti-aircraft gun being dug in.*

Aircraft piloted by Old Brightonians

Vickers Wellington bombers over the Western Desert, 1942 (see Peter Torkington-Leech, Raymond Elliott, Charles Young, Derek Normington and Charles O'Connor, pages 27, 38, 65, 86 and 153).

Hurricane fighter over England (see Leonid Ereminsky, page 36).

Blenheim bomber over the North Sea, 1940 (see Philip Hemsley, Alexander Morton, Gerald Clayton and Phillip Gibbs, pages 26, 28, 39 and 53).

Hampden bomber over Scotland, 1942 (see Konstantine Ballas-Andersen, John Oldfield, Ernest Davis and Peter Close, pages 41, 45, 66 and 76).

Hawker Hart bomber over England (see George Watson, page 67).

Armourers at Mildenhall in Suffolk poised to load a Short Stirling with bombs for a night raid on Essen, Germany (see John Holdsworth and Raymond Belcher, pages 88 and 138).

Avro Lancaster bombers over England on 29 September 1942 (see Richard Bayldon, Eliot Welchman and Roger Ward, pages 125, 143 and 150).

A Martin Baltimore bomber from 223 Squadron dropping bombs during a raid on the railway station and junction at Sulmona, Italy (see William Baillie, page 119).

Boston III light bomber and reconnaissance aircraft flying an air test over Egypt in 1941 (see Lionel Baily, page 134).

Handley Page Halifax bomber over England, 1944 (see John Trehearn and George Russel, pages 116 and 141).

Lockheed Hudson bomber and reconnaissance aircraft off the Scottish coast, 1942 (see Henry Featherstone and John Allen, page 52).

Midshipman Francis Hugh Twycross-Raines RN (Walpole and Bristol Houses 1933–35)

Killed in action off the Egyptian coast on 25 November 1941, aged 20

Francis was born on 3 June 1921 to Francis Twycross-Raines and his wife Dorothy (née Mckintoch). He attended Brighton College for two years, playing minor roles in the Gilbert and Sullivan operettas *The Gondoliers* and *The Sorcerer*, before switching to the Specialist Army Class at Dulwich College. From there he went to Dartmouth College to train as a naval officer.

By November 1941 he was on the battleship HMS *Barham*, part of a battle squadron (1st Battle Squadron) looking for Italian convoys. A U-boat discovered the group of British ships on the mission just off the Egyptian coast, and hit the *Barham* with three torpedoes. The ship rapidly began to capsize to port and four minutes later her magazines exploded, shattering the entire ship in an enormous explosion. Twycross-Raines was among the two-thirds of the crew who were lost with the ship. His name is inscribed on the Portsmouth War Memorial.

Top: *Francis Hugh Twycross-Raines.*

Above: *HMS* Barham *explodes as her magazine ignites, 25 November 1941.*

Captain William David Yeo
(Stenning and Wilson's Houses 1930–35)

Died on active service in Libya on 26 November 1941, aged 24

William was born on 9 March 1917 to Colonel Herbert Yeo and his wife Dorothy. At the College he was an all-rounder: School Prefect, Platoon Commander in the Officer Training Corps, member of the swimming and water polo teams, and winner of prizes in French and Classics.

During the war William served with the 1st Royal Tank Regiment, and died on active service in Libya during Operation *Crusader*, the successful attempt by the Allies to end the siege of Tobruk. Yeo left a widow, Joyce, and is buried at the Tobruk War Cemetery.

Captain John Ramsay Paton (Durnford House 1933–38)

Died of wounds in Malaya on 19 December 1941, aged 22

It was always likely that John Paton would choose a career in the military as he was the son of an army officer, Ramsay Paton, and grandson of Sergeant Major William Paton, one of the heroes who saved the guns from the Afghans at the Battle of Maiwand in 1880.

Born on 12 July 1919 in Farnham, Surrey, to Marianne Paton (née Bowring), John represented the school in the Shooting VIII and Boxing VIII, fighting as a 'slight but plucky' paperweight with an excellent straight left. He also won prizes for English and Geography.

In 1938 he trained as an officer at Sandhurst. On passing out he joined the 13th Frontier Rifles of the Indian Army, which, as Britain's war in Asia began in 1941, found itself attacked by Japanese forces in Malaya.

On 18 December Japanese forces ambushed three of his battalion's armoured carriers while they were on patrol. Paton was part of the force detailed to retrieve them, but was mortally wounded in the fighting, and died in hospital a day later. On the day of his death, when his Sikh orderly had remonstrated with him for exposing himself to danger unnecessarily, he had laughingly replied that the Japanese had not made the bullet that would kill him. Describing the incident, his commanding officer wrote afterwards:

> Paton was put on a stretcher, wonderfully brave and cheerful, so much so in fact that I did not realize how seriously he had been hit.

Paton is buried in the Taiping War Cemetery in Perak, Malaysia.

Top: *Captain William David Yeo.*

Above: *Captain John Ramsay Paton.*

1942

Dawson family photograph, 1933, with Canon William Dawson, Head Master, in the centre. Michael Dawson (see page 86) is third from left. Paul Dawson (see page 146) is at the rear, on the right.

Pilot Officer Peter Thrale Close (School House 1923–26)

Killed when his plane came down off France on 10 January 1942, aged 32

Peter was born in Holborn, Middlesex, on 21 May 1909, the son of Rev. Herbert Close, a vicar, and his wife Olive (née Thrale). His father was teaching at the College when Peter entered the Junior School – this was a time when public school masters were much more commonly in holy orders than now. At some point after leaving the College Peter went to South Africa for a time, and by 1939 was a headmaster's secretary, living in Croydon, Surrey.

During the war he served as an air observer in 49 Squadron flying the Hampden bomber, known as the Flying Suitcase because of its cramped conditions. He was based at RAF Scampton in Lincolnshire.

Close's aircraft went missing while flying a mine-laying mission near the French port of Brest on 10 January 1942. The mission was designed to hem in the German battlecruisers *Scharnhorst* and *Gneisenau*, and the heavy cruiser *Prinz Eugen*, the month before their famed 'Channel Dash', an attempt to relocate to Norway to counter a possible British invasion of the country. Although minesweepers secretly cleared a way for them, allowing the ships to escape, the ships only made it as far as Germany. Close's body was never recovered, and his name is inscribed on the Runnymede Air Forces Memorial.

Lieutenant Ralph Edward Arthur Stebbing (Stenning House 1926–29)

Died on active service in Malaya on 25 January 1942, aged 29

Ralph was born on 15 September 1912 in Bromley, Kent, to Sydney Stebbing and his wife Dora (née Rogers). At the College he played the flute in two Gilbert and Sullivan operettas: *The Gondoliers* and *The Mikado*. In 1938 he married Margaret Aston, the rather intimidatingly titled Instructress in the Women's League of Health and Beauty, at Shirley Parish Church in Surrey. The wedding party was so fetching that the nuptials were commemorated with a headline and photo on the front page of the *Sevenoaks Chronicle*, depicting 11 other women from the League standing around them in uniform.

During the war Ralph served as a lieutenant in the 135th (Hertfordshire Yeomanry) Field Regiment of the Royal Artillery. The regiment remained in the United Kingdom until 1941, when it was deployed to defend Singapore. Stebbing was caught up in the successful Japanese invasion of Malaya, to the north of Singapore, and died on active service 12 days after arriving. He is buried in the Taiping War Cemetery in Malaya.

Top: Pilot Officer Peter Thrale Close.

Above: Lieutenant Ralph Edward Arthur Stebbing.

Lieutenant John Evelyn Desmond Darwall RN
(Walpole House 1931–34)

Died of disease in Malaya on
26 January 1942, aged 24

Born on 5 December 1917 to Commander William Darwall, a retired Royal Navy officer decorated with the DSO, and his wife Eda, known as Elaine, John trained as a naval cadet after leaving the College, becoming a midshipman in 1935 and serving with the naval branch of the Royal Engineers.

By the outbreak of war he was on HMS *Repulse*, a battlecruiser. The *Repulse* and the battleship she was accompanying, HMS *Prince of Wales*, were sunk in the South China Sea by Japanese bombers on 10 December 1941, a mere three days after Japan had entered the war. Darwall, picked up by the destroyer *Electra*, was among the survivors. He was despatched forthwith to Malaya to take command of a party of men patrolling the coast, running trains and carrying out demolitions to impede the Japanese advance. While engaged in these duties – much of the time, probably, in the disease-ridden jungle – he became ill and soon after died of meningoencephalitis. Darwall is buried at the Kranji War Cemetery in Singapore.

Top: *Newly arrived British troops give the thumbs up on the quayside at Singapore, November 1941; this is a particularly poignant image, considering what was to come.*

Above: *Lieutenant John Evelyn Desmond Darwall.*

Lieutenant John Stanley Noel Myles
(Wilson's and Chichester Houses 1933–36)

Killed in action in Singapore on 10 February 1942, aged 22

John Myles, known as Billy, was born in Singapore on 16 June 1919 to Daisy and Jack Myles. He enlisted in the Indian Army, and was assigned to the 18th Royal Garhwal Rifles. When the Japanese invaded Malaya in 1941, his regiment became involved in the dispiriting rout of the Allied forces.

It was a strange time. Billy encountered a 'suicide squad' of Japanese soldiers who pedalled furiously on bicycles towards his position, to be killed to a man when his unit opened fire. A huge Japanese force then swarmed down, having discovered the exact position of the enemy troops and guns. At another point, after the Allied forces had been forced to retreat to the island of Singapore, Billy and three comrades went to the famous Raffles Hotel for a drink, to find a band playing but only two other occupied tables, around which sat, according to one of his comrades, 'a few dirty, unshaven, tired army officers'. The party then broke up when two military policemen told the four of them to return to units immediately, in line with orders that had just come in that evening.

By 10 February 1942 the Japanese had begun to fight their way through the plantations on the island. The following day the same comrade recounted the tale of Billy's death in a rubber plantation, saying:

> Billy had gone forward with the Colonel, the Signals Officer and several others to reconnoitre a Japanese position in a wood. They were spotted by the Japs and in his haste to withdraw, the driver stalled the jeep. The Japs opened fire and they were all killed instantly. For good measure, the Japs flung a few hand grenades into the jeep. Billy was buried near the junction of Thomson Rd and Mandai Road.

Lieutenant-Colonel Ian Conway Gifford Lywood
(School House 1914–17)

Murdered in hospital in Singapore in February 1942, aged 42

Ian was born on 10 September 1899 in Blantyre, Lanarkshire, Scotland, to Edwin Lywood, the scion of a farming family who later became a lieutenant-colonel in the Royal Marines, and his wife Ethel (née Wells). Ian joined the Royal Norfolk Regiment during the Great War and stayed on in peacetime, rising up the ranks. By February 1942 he was a lieutenant-colonel in charge of the regiment's 2nd Battalion.

Top: *Lieutenant John Stanley Noel Myles.*

Above: *Ian Conway Gifford Lywood, in the 1917 School House photograph.*

Lywood was murdered in hospital by the Japanese when Singapore fell to the Japanese, on 14 or 15 February 1942, and was among the first of thousands of Britons to fall prey to Japanese military atrocities during the war. He is buried at Singapore's Kranji Military Cemetery.

Second Lieutenant Laurence Pontifex Sly (Hampden B House 1928–33)

Died on active service in Singapore on 15 February 1942, aged 26

The exotically named Laurence Pontifex Sly (a pontifex was an ancient Roman high priest) was born in Reigate, Surrey, on 24 March 1915, the son of Harold Sly, a stockbroker, and his wife Mildred (née Shattock). Laurence attended the College on an exhibition, and won the Lower Fifth English prize. He rose eventually to be Head of House, editor of the school magazine and Under Officer in the Officer Training Corps.

On leaving school he worked for a trading company involved in rubber plantations in Malaya, where in September 1941 he was commissioned as a second lieutenant in the Armoured Car Regiment. He died on active service during the fall of Singapore to the Japanese on 15 February 1942 and is commemorated on the Singapore Memorial.

Commander Cecil Wakeford May RN (Durnford House 1912–17)

Killed when his ship was sunk in the Java Sea on 27 February 1942, aged 42

Cecil was born on 1 June 1899 in Twickenham, Middlesex, to Hermon May, a solicitor, and his wife Ethel (née Harris). We have no direct information about what he did in the years between his time at the College, where he was a House Prefect and a member of the Shooting VIII, and the Second World War. However, he had doubtless already served many years in the Royal Navy before the outbreak of war, because at the end of 1940 he was given command of his own destroyer, HMS *Electra*, with the rank of lieutenant-commander. In 1941 the ship saved men from the battlecruiser *Repulse*, including fellow Old Brightonian John Darwall (see page 77), after she was sunk by Japanese planes.

In February 1942 the *Electra* was sunk by Japanese surface ships in the Battle of the Java Sea, a major Japanese victory. In correspondence with the College almost a year later, his mother wrote:

> Two of the crew have written me the most awfully nice letters and all the men seemed very devoted to their Captain.

Cecil left a widow, Eileen, and is commemorated at the Chatham Naval Memorial in Kent.

■ Above: *1912 Durnford House photograph.*

Conflicts in the Far East

Above: The Prince of Wales *(upper ship in background)* and Repulse *(lower ship in background) are attacked by Japanese planes, 10 December 1941.*

Left: *A 1943 painting showing prisoners of war carrying a log across the River Kwai in Thailand.*

Below: *Troops of 5th Indian Division loading a jeep into a Douglas Dakota Mark III of 194 Squadron RAF during the reinforcement of the Imphal Garrison in India, 1944.*

Above: *Lieutenant-General Arthur Percival on his way to surrender Singapore to the Japanese, 15 February 1942.*

Right: *Convalescent prisoners repairing boots in a prisoner-of-war camp on the Burma–Siam Railway.*

Below: *Poster for the 1957 film* The Bridge on the River Kwai.

Private Edwin Ronald Dodd Hatt
(Wilson's House 1925–27)

Died in a prisoner-of-war camp in or near Singapore on 1 March 1942, aged 30

Edwin Hatt was born on 30 June 1911 to Edwin Hatt, a solicitor, and his wife Mary (née Dodd). A keen sportsman and athlete who played rugby, cricket, hockey and football, he was instantly put in a number of 1st teams after joining Brighton College in 1925. Before the war, Hatt worked as an estate agent in London.

He joined the East Surrey Regiment in July 1940, and was sent to Singapore about a year later. His unit was part of the 80,000-strong Allied forces that surrendered with the fall of Singapore to the Japanese in February 1942. He died in a diphtheria epidemic shortly after the surrender and is buried in the Commonwealth War Graves Commission Cemetery in Singapore.

Reginald Lewis 'Rex' Nunn, DSO
(Junior School and School House 1902–09)

Drowned after his ship was torpedoed in the Indian Ocean on 1 March 1942, aged 49

Rex was born on 11 September 1892 to Albert Nunn, an engineer, and his wife Frances, of Tenterden, Kent. At the College he excelled at shooting and was an enthusiastic rather than talented footballer – according to a match report in the school magazine, he was 'painfully slow although he did try extremely hard'.

During the Great War Rex served in the Royal Marines Divisional Engineers, rising to the rank of major, and was awarded the Distinguished Service Order in the last year of the war. After the war he built a flourishing career, rising to become Director of Public Works and Director of Civil Aviation in the British colony of Malaya, based in Singapore. He was very happily married to Gertrude Higgs, a celebrated choral and opera singer.

When the Japanese invaded Singapore, Rex organised the evacuation of many personnel from his department, and was among the last to leave the island. The first ship on which Rex and his wife embarked was sunk by Japanese bombers, but they both made it to Pom Pong Island, where they were rescued by the SS Rooseboom, as was fellow Old Brightonian John Acworth (see page 84). Unfortunately, this ship was torpedoed by the Japanese. The couple were below decks, but Rex saved his wife's life by breaking through a porthole and lifting her through. Rex drowned, and Gertrude died eight days later on a lifeboat, starved of food and water, talking about her beloved husband to the end.

Above: *Private Edwin Ronald Dodd Hatt.* ∎

Group Captain George Frederick Whistondale (School House 1921–24)

Killed in action in the Dutch East Indies on 1 March 1942, aged 34

George was born on 2 June 1907 to Frederick Whistondale and his Norwegian-born wife, Eliza (née Knutsen). After Brighton College, where he was part of the debating team, he joined the RAF. In 1936 he married Annie Woodrow.

Whistondale died on 1 March 1942 when Kalidjati airfield in Java in the Dutch East Indies was overrun by the Japanese. He was the commanding officer at the airfield at the time and was last seen returning to his office, reportedly to retrieve his stamp collection. Whistondale's car was ambushed and he and his passenger were killed. He is commemorated on the Singapore Memorial.

Top: *Group photograph of 'Miss Diana Shelley's friends', 1931. Reginald Nunn is sitting on the far left, next to the man holding the camera.*

Above: *Group Captain George Frederick Whistondale.*

Lieutenant-Colonel John Pelham Acworth (Hampden House 1915)

Died somewhere at sea between Sumatra and Ceylon on 3 March 1942, aged 44

John was born on the last day of 1897 in Milton Regis, Kent, to Emily and Amos Acworth. On leaving the College he decided to join the Indian Army, working as a deckhand on a boat to the country to pay his way, and was commissioned as a second lieutenant with the Poona Horse Regiment. His first battle experience was in 1917 at Cambrai in northern France, when mounted soldiers fought alongside the newfangled tanks that would soon completely supplant horses in warfare.

In 1919 Acworth served as a squadron commander in the Third Anglo-Afghan War, serving in Baluchistan (now in south-west Pakistan) where he learned the local language, Baluchi. Acworth disguised himself as a beggar to listen to all the gossip around the marketplaces, thus gaining valuable information regarding the poisoning of wells and possible ambush sites for the next season's army expeditions. There is a splendid photo of him in this garb, though with his erect military posture he is distinctly un-beggar like (see page 16).

In 1929 Acworth, by now a captain, returned to England for officer training at Sandhurst. While in England he met and married Jean Wallace, who bore him a son, Hugh, later a major in the British Army, and a daughter, Caroline.

In May 1941 he was promoted to lieutenant-colonel in command of the 4th Battalion of the 12th Frontier Force Regiment, part of the 11th Indian Division. Based in the British colony of Malaya, the division suffered huge casualties when the Japanese attacked in December 1941, and surrendered in February 1942 when Singapore fell to the Japanese. Acworth managed to escape to Sumatra in the Dutch East Indies, where he boarded the SS *Rooseboom* (which also rescued fellow Old Brightonian Rex Nunn – see page 82), sailing for the British colony of Ceylon. However, on 1 March 1942 the ship was sunk by a Japanese submarine and managed to launch only one lifeboat, built to carry 28 but with 135 souls crowded onto it.

Far from panicking, Acworth came into his own. He took charge of rationing and decreed that every fit man was to do a spell of four hours per day in the water. However, when the boat ran aground 26 days later near Sumatra, after much suffering and one case of cannibalism, there were only four survivors – and Acworth was not among them. Acworth is commemorated at the Singapore Memorial.

Above: *John Acworth marries Jean Wallace, 1931.* ▪

Flying Officer Gerald Gordon Lonsdale (Hampden House 1930–34)

Killed in a plane crash over the Atlantic on 24 April 1942, aged 25

Gerald Lonsdale was born on 13 June 1916 in Willesden, London, to Harry Lonsdale, who worked in insurance, and his wife Cicely (née Villiers). After leaving Brighton College, where he was a keen sportsman, Gerald became a bank clerk in Brighton, and married Marjorie Aiken a couple of years later in 1936.

Gerald enlisted in the RAF in July 1940. Within six months he had obtained his commission, and was serving with Coastal Command, which attacked enemy shipping and protected Allied vessels. In November 1941 his unit, 502 (Ulster) Squadron, was the first in Coastal Command to sink a U-boat.

On 24 April 1942 he was in charge of an aircraft on patrol in the Bay of Biscay when he signalled that he was returning with engine trouble. He almost made it, but when he was 20–30 miles south of the Isles of Scilly, he sent an SOS and then nothing else was heard. His plane was never found. Gerald is commemorated on a plaque at St Andrew's Church in Edburton, West Sussex.

Flying Officer George Cornelius Buxton (School House 1935–39)

Killed in an aircraft accident in England on 28 April 1942, aged 21

George Cornelius Buxton was born on 4 March 1921 to George Buxton and his wife Ellen (née Sawtill) of Scaynes Hill in West Sussex. At Brighton College he had a varied sporting career as a stalwart of both the water polo team and the 1st XV, and became Head of House.

During the war Buxton served in the RAF, flying the Lockheed Hudson bomber. On 28 April 1942 he was approaching RAF Cranage in Cheshire when his aircraft spun into the ground, killing all six on board. He is buried close to the crash site, in Saint John's Church, Byley. Buxton had been promoted to flying officer just the previous day.

Top: *Flying Officer Gerald Gordon Lonsdale.*

Above: *Flying Officer George Cornelius Buxton.*

Pilot Officer Michael Anthony Rodgers Dawson (School House 1924–29)

Died of gunshot wounds in Egypt on 18 May 1942, aged 31

Michael Dawson was born in Brighton on 20 June 1910, the son of Frances Dawson (née Sykes) and Canon William Dawson, Head Master of Brighton College, and younger brother of Paul (see page 146). After attending the College, where he became Head of House, he read English Literature at Oriel College, Oxford.

When war began Dawson was stationed in Greece with the British Council. In reality, he was working for the intelligence services, according to his brother, recruited because of his facility with languages. When the Germans invaded Greece in 1941 Dawson only just made it out, and joined the RAF as a pilot officer. Dawson died of gunshot wounds on 18 May 1942 in Egypt, and is buried at the Heliopolis War Cemetery in Cairo.

Sergeant Derek Harry Normington (Durnford House 1933–36)

Missing, presumed killed, in a bombing raid over Germany on 30 May 1942, aged 22

Derek Normington was born on 20 November 1919 in Richmond, Surrey, to Florence and Alfred Normington, an insurance broker. After leaving the College in 1936 he served in the Royal Air Force Volunteer Reserve.

By 1942, Normington was attached to 156 Squadron, based at RAF Alconbury, Cambridgeshire, as a wireless operator and air gunner. On the night of 31 May 1942 he took part in the first of the famous 'thousand bomber raids' on Germany, attacking Cologne. The majority of the bombers, including Normington's own machine, were Wellingtons. Normington's plane failed to return and he was reported missing, presumed killed on active service. Writing to Walter Hett, Head Master of the College, his father said:

I can assure you it is the worst tragedy of my life, which I feel acutely.

The Germans confirmed later that year that he had been killed and he is buried in the Bergen-op-Zoom War Cemetery in the Netherlands.

Top: *Pilot Officer Michael Anthony Rodgers Dawson.*

Above: *Sergeant Derek Harry Normington.*

Flying Officer David Dudley Plaister Joyce RCAF (Chichester House 1933–36)

Killed when his aircraft was shot down over Germany on 2 June 1942, aged 23

David Joyce was born on 25 May 1919 and grew up in Buenos Aires, Argentina. He was the son of Evelyn and Dudley Joyce, Britons who had settled in the country; and his father was a civil engineer. At Brighton College Joyce became a Prefect and was both academic and sporty, being selected for the 1st XI and 1st XV. Returning home to Argentina, he joined the Buenos Aires cricket and rugby clubs.

On the outbreak of war Joyce initially served on the Falkland Islands Defence Force, a small group of Anglo-Argentine volunteers formed to defend the islands from attack by German raiders. He may have been recruited by personal friends as many of the small group played rugby with each other back in Argentina. In October 1940 Joyce joined the Canadian Royal Air Force, having doubtless emigrated to Canada at an earlier point. He became a pilot officer with 10 Squadron, which flew bombers.

On the night of 1/2 June 1942 his plane was hit by anti-aircraft fire while on a bombing mission targeting the German city of Essen. Badly damaged, it crashed, with the loss of Joyce and five other crew members, though one survived to become a prisoner of war. Joyce and his comrades are buried in Reichswald Forest War Cemetery.

Top: *A mass bomber raid on Cologne. Painting by W. Krogman.*

Above: *Flying Officer David Dudley Plaister Joyce.*

Captain Hector Alexander Findlater Graham (School House 1927–31)

Died on active service in India on 6 June 1942, aged 29

Hector Graham was born on 16 May 1913, the only child of Alexander Graham and his wife Mary (née Findlater), who lived in Islington, London. Hector had a distinguished time at the College, winning two modern languages prizes, taking part in debating, and representing the school in cross-country running. He also passed the written examination for Certificate 'A' in the Officer Training Corps tests.

In 1937 he enlisted as a private in the London Scottish Regiment, representing his company when it was visited by King George VI and Queen Elizabeth. In 1942, serving with the Reconnaissance Corps, he died on active service in Bombay. As the city was far from the front, he may well have succumbed to disease. After his death, a comrade remembered, in the *Daily Telegraph*, first meeting him three years before:

A cheerful, upstanding, smart looking lad, it struck us that he was the right type for an officer.

He is buried at the Kirkee War Cemetery.

Pilot Officer John Barry Holdsworth RAFVR (Durnford House 1935–38)

Crashed into the sea off the Netherlands on 7 June 1942, aged 21

John Holdsworth was born on 28 September 1920 to Gilbert Holdsworth and his wife Adelaide (née Chambers). At the College he was House Prefect and in the Swimming VIII.

During the war he flew first in Wellingtons and then in Short Stirling bombers for 214 Squadron, based at RAF Stradishall. He was lucky to survive the disastrous raid by the squadron on the railway yards at Hanau in Germany on the night of 1/2 April 1942, when it lost seven planes, but was killed two months later on a mission to bomb Emden, crashing into the sea off Terschelling, an island off the Dutch mainland. His elder brother Frank (see page 159) died three years later, also while serving in the RAF. Holdsworth is commemorated at the Runnymede Air Forces Memorial.

Top: *Captain Hector Alexander Findlater Graham.*
Above: *John Barry Holdsworth, in the 1937 Durnford House photograph.*

Second Lieutenant Philip Ernest Groves
(Wilson's House 1928–32)

Killed in action in Libya on 20 June 1942, aged 28

Philip Groves was born on 31 March 1914 in Leeds, Yorkshire, to Ernest Groves, a schoolmaster, and his wife Gertrude (née Blackwell). Philip was known at the College as 'Shakespeare', which suggests a literary inclination, and won a prize for German. Nevertheless, after leaving the College he took a BSc at Imperial College, London, before setting off to Asia to become a geologist with the Burma Oil Company, prospecting for oil. A letter written to the school by his brother after Philip's death suggests a distant relationship with his family, since his brother notes that the family did not see him in the last six years of his life.

In 1940 Groves joined the Royal Artillery. He was posted first to Iraq, and then to the desert campaign in North Africa. In June 1942 he died of wounds incurred in Libya, and is buried there at the Knightsbridge War Cemetery.

Lieutenant Gordon Francis Elliott
(Durnford House 1933–36)

Killed in action in Egypt on 28 June 1942, aged 23

Gordon was born on 1 December 1918 to Harold Elliott, a dentist who had served in the army in the Great War, and his wife Gladys (née Way) of Steyning, near Brighton. At the College he was a member of the Shooting VIII.

When war came he enlisted in the 2nd Battalion of the Cheshire Regiment, and participated in the Battle for France in 1940, before being evacuated from Dunkirk. He then fought in the Western Desert campaign and was killed in Egypt in June 1942. Elliott is buried at the El Alamein War Cemetery. His older brother, Raymond (see page 38), was lost on the return flight from a bombing mission over Germany in 1940.

Top: *Knightsbrigde War Cemetery, Acroma, Libya.*

Above: *Lieutenant Gordon Francis Elliott.*

North African Campaign, 1941–43

Top: British soldiers lie in a tent playing cards, *by Frank C. Ward, 1943.*

Middle: *A British Crusader tank passes a burning German Pzkw Mk IV tank during Operation Crusader, 26 November 1941.*

Bottom: *Australian troops fraternise with British soldiers of the 8th Army shortly after arriving at El Alamein, 13 July 1942.*

A 1942 wartime desert landscape *by Edward Jeffrey Irving Ardizzone.*

German and Italian prisoners at Gromalia prisoner-of-war camp after the May 1943 fall of Tunis.

Flight Lieutenant Alfred Fleming RAFVR
(School House 1928–30)

Went missing over the Bay of Biscay on 10 July 1942, aged 28

Alfred was born on 13 January 1914 in Portsmouth, to Alfred Fleming, Fellow of the Royal Society of Arts and a fine art and antiques dealer with shops in Portsmouth and Pall Mall Place, London, and his wife Louisa (née Roberton). After leaving the College Fleming joined the family business, while playing rugby for Hampshire and serving for a while as captain of the famous Portsmouth Rugby Football Club. The Fleming firm supplied, among others, Queen Mary, wife of George V, and the National Maritime Museum in Greenwich. In 1938 Fleming married Ivy Kerridge.

In March 1939, six months before the war began, Fleming opted to join the Royal Air Force Volunteer Reserve, perhaps with a presentiment that he might be needed. He was commissioned as a pilot officer in late 1940, flying the Bristol Blenheim bomber with 53 Squadron. In only five months he completed 31 sorties, attacking German torpedo boats, submarine pens and other targets in occupied France. He also twice participated in an attack on the *Admiral Hipper*, a German heavy cruiser, in Brest harbour.

In 1941 he was transferred to 58 Squadron, flying the Whitley bomber on missions over Germany, France and the Netherlands, and was promoted to flight lieutenant. Late in the year Fleming volunteered for 138 Squadron, a Special Duties Squadron that dropped special forces into occupied France and undertook secret operations in the Middle and Far East. He then rejoined 58 Squadron, now tasked with patrolling the seas as part of Coastal Command.

Above: *'A' Flight during training at RAF Andover, September 1940. Alfred Fleming is in the middle row, second from left.*

In June 1942, he was offered the prestigious post of aide-de-camp to the governor of Gibraltar, but he turned it down to continue flying in a combat role for 58 Squadron. On 10 July he took off from his base at St Eval in Cornwall to fly an anti-submarine patrol over the Bay of Biscay, but never returned from this, his 50th operational mission.

Fleming received the Air Crew Europe Star campaign medal, and is commemorated on one of the panels at the RAF Memorial at Runnymede. The Memorial remembers 20,455 air force personnel who perished in the war without a known grave, with the collective inscription: 'Their name liveth for evermore'. He was survived by his wife Ivy and their son Alfred, and by an older and a younger brother, fellow Old Brightonians who both survived the war after serving with distinction.

Captain William Anthony Palmer, MC
(School House 1933–37)

Killed in action in Egypt on 23 July 1942, aged 23

William, known as Tony to his friends, was born in Paris on 5 June 1919 to Morris Palmer, assistant manager of the Paris branch of Westminster Bank, and his wife Lilah (née Bishop). At the College he was in the top swimming and boxing teams, with a strong fight record at House level. Moving on to Sandhurst to train as an officer, he earned a Level 1 Translator's Certificate in French.

On 30 December 1941 he received a Military Cross for organising a successful counter-attack against superior numbers by the company he was commanding, while serving with the 14th Punjab Regiment of the Indian Army. The citation lauded Palmer, at this point a lieutenant, for 'showing the highest qualities of leadership, coolness in action, and determination'. Palmer was killed in the First Battle of El Alamein, in July 1942, and is buried in the El Alamein War Cemetery.

THE MILITARY CROSS

LIEUTENANT WILLIAM ANTHONY PALMER

14th Punjab Regiment, Indian Army

On July 14th, 1941, Lieutenant W. A. Palmer was in command of a company which was covering the withdrawal of the Battalion from a position north-west of Debarach.

This officer, when his company position was heavily attacked by superior numbers of the enemy, and when one of his forward platoon positions had been overrun, showed the highest qualities of leadership, coolness in action, and determination, and by personal example so encouraged his men that a counter attack organised and led by him was entirely successful and the enemy put completely to flight, leaving some ten to fifteen dead on the field and one L.M.G. in the hands of his Company.

AN "EPITAPH" FROM HIS REGIMENT :

"He was a grand, likeable boy and did very very well for the Regiment, gaining an M.C. and a Mention in Despatches. He died on July 23rd, leading his Company in the attack."

Above: *Captain William Anthony Palmer, MC.*

Above, right: *The July 1943 edition of the* Brightonian *magazine relates the story of how William Palmer came to be awarded the Military Cross.*

Flying Officer Anthony John Lee Bowes RAFVR (Common Room 1936–37)

Killed when his aircraft was shot down over the Netherlands on 24 July 1942, aged 28

Anthony John Lee Bowes, known as 'Johnnie', was born on 8 October 1913 into a family of GPs in Herne Bay, Kent, and was the son of Tom Bowes MD and his wife Gertrude (née Lee). Anthony won the top scholarship to Charterhouse School, where he eventually became a Head of House. He then won a scholarship to read Classics at Christ Church, Oxford, where he sang in the Bach Choir.

Bowes decided to become a schoolmaster, taking his first job after graduation at Brighton College. Despite his brief time at the College, Bowes made his mark, according to Vaughan Harris, an Oxford contemporary who joined the staff of the College at the same time. He played Bach's cantata 'Jesu Joy of Man's Desiring' at a concert in the Great Hall, and engendered, according to Harris, 'affection and enthusiasm in the boys who came under his care'.

During this time he made a name for himself as an entomologist, amassing a collection of more than 10,000 moths and butterflies, which is now at the Natural History Museum. He had just received a firm job offer to teach at Eton when in 1940, at the age of 27, he was called up to the RAF and commissioned into 149 Squadron, which flew night bombers.

On 13 July 1942 Bowes was posted to 149 Squadron, based at RAF Lakenheath in Suffolk. On 24 July, he took off in a Stirling bomber to participate in a raid on Duisburg in Germany. The plane was shot down by a German night-fighter over the Netherlands, probably on its way home after the raid. In a short but eloquent letter to his parents, written days before his death and imbued with his Christian faith, Bowes quoted the poet Shelley and finished with the sentence:

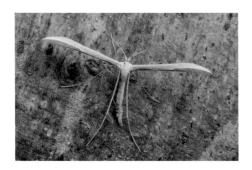

And thank you for so full a life: you have been far too good for me, and far too good to me.

He is buried in Uden War Cemetery, in the Netherlands.

In a touching postscript to Bowes' life, 18 years after his death the entomologist Paul Whalley described a new kind of moth on examining Bowes' collection in the British Museum. The species, *Oidematophorus bowesi Whalley*, was named after him.

Top: *Flying Officer Anthony John Lee Bowes.*

Above: *Image of the moth* Oidematophorus bowesi Whalley *(now known as* Hellinsia chrysocomae – *Scarce Goldenrod Plume).*

Flight Lieutenant Douglas Weston Whiteman (Bristol House 1932–35)

Killed when his aircraft was shot down over Germany on 29 July 1942, aged 23

Douglas Whiteman was born on 24 September 1918 in Cawnpore, Bengal, in India, and was the only child of Alice Whiteman (née Smith), daughter of a soldier, and William Whiteman, a second lieutenant in the Royal Artillery.

By 1932 his family had returned to London, and in that year Whiteman joined Bristol House. After his death his parents wrote to the Head Master declaring 'how proud he was of being an Old Brightonian'.

Whiteman joined the RAF in January 1939. He spent almost three years in Egypt prior to serving in Europe, where he piloted a Stirling bomber as part of 7 Squadron. On 29 July 1942 Whiteman took part in an RAF air raid on Hamburg, but was shot down. He met a heroic end. Three crew members from his aircraft who bailed out and survived to become prisoners of war wrote to his parents explaining that after the plane was hit by anti-aircraft fire, Whiteman, who commanded the plane, gave orders for them to bail out. Whiteman and the navigator remained in the aircraft to try to get the badly wounded wireless operator out, but they did not make it before it crashed. It was a double tragedy as he was due to come home the next day to marry, though we do not know his fiancée's name.

It took two years for his family to learn for sure that he had been killed, but in September 1944 his parents wrote to the school saying that after hoping that he had been taken prisoner along with his comrades, they had finally been informed the previous month that he was officially deemed dead. Whiteman is buried in Becklingen War Cemetery.

Kenneth Gordon Seth-Smith (School House 1928–31)

Killed in a test flight in England on 11 August 1942, aged 28

Kenneth was born in Caterham Valley, Surrey, on 13 July 1914 to Gordon Seth-Smith and his wife Margaret (née Stedman). A need for speed was in his blood: his father was a pioneering motorist, and the couple's honeymoon was a round-Britain tour in a single-cylinder Star car.

Seth-Smith won a Mathematics prize at the College, and also appeared as Edith, one of General Stanley's daughters, in *The Pirates of Penzance*. After leaving the College he became an accountant for a short while. However, this was very much his

Top: *Flight Lieutenant Douglas Weston Whiteman.*

Above: *Kenneth Gordon Seth-Smith.*

family's idea rather than his own, and he soon switched to General Aircraft, a civil aircraft manufacturer, starting as an apprentice and gradually rising through the ranks to become manager. In 1938 he married Joy Tobin, a 17-year-old drama student at RADA. Their only child, Richard, who was born the following year, says that his parents were deeply in love but ultimately knew that the war could easily take one of them away so, like many other young couples of the time, they married quickly.

Kenneth's life assuredly became more dangerous the following year, when he became a test pilot with the Hawker Aircraft Company, which produced iconic Second World War planes including the Hurricane and Spitfire. On 11 August 1942 he was carrying out a speed test in a Hawker Typhoon when his aircraft broke up over the Surrey countryside, killing him. His son Richard followed in his father's footsteps by running a flying school at Perranporth in Cornwall.

Sub-Lieutenant Brian Stanley Sargent RNVR (Bristol House 1934–39)

Killed in action off France on 19 August 1942, aged 22

Brian Sargent was born on 1 August 1920 to Stanley Sargent, a jobber on the London Stock Exchange, and his wife Kate (née Ablitt). After boarding at Bristol House, he joined the Royal Naval Volunteer Reserve, and became an acting sub-lieutenant. We do not know anything about his war service until the battle in which he died: the Dieppe Raid of 19 August 1942, when Allied troops launched an attack on the German-occupied French port, partly to gather intelligence but mostly to learn lessons ahead of a full-scale invasion of France. Sargent was serving on HMS *Glengyle*, a cargo ship converted into a landing craft. The ship was sunk by enemy fire, along with 32 other landing craft, and he was killed. He is commemorated at the Portsmouth Naval Memorial.

Top: *Photograph of the Brighton College production of* The Pirates of Penzance, *December 1929.*

Above: *Sub-Lieutenant Brian Stanley Sargent's entry in the College Roll of Honour.*

Francis Lakin Mansel (Walpole House 1922–25)

Murdered by the Japanese military in the Dutch East Indies on 27 August 1942, aged 34

Francis was born on 8 May 1908 in Oakengates, Shropshire, to Edward Mansel, an architect. After leaving the College he went out to the British colony of Sarawak, now part of Malaysia, as a civil servant working in the Treasury in Sarawak. In 1941 the Japanese invaded the colony and he fled to Long Nawang in the Dutch East Indies. However, the following year the Japanese took this colony too, and Mansel was murdered by the occupying forces. It is believed that he is buried locally.

Captain Paul Crinks (Stenning House 1930–32)

Killed in action in Egypt on 27 October 1942, aged 26

Paul was born in Bristol on 22 November 1915, the son of Percival Crinks, an electrical engineer, and his wife Ethel (née Fielding). He served with the Royal Tank Regiment in the Western Desert campaign, where tanks reigned supreme in the open desert terrain. He was killed in Egypt in the first few days of the Second Battle of El Alamein. Ultimate victory in this battle marked the death knell of the Axis presence in North Africa in the spring of 1943. After the battle Churchill famously said:

> Before Alamein we never had a victory.
> After Alamein we never had a defeat.

He is buried at the El Alamein War Cemetery.

Top: *Francis Lakin Mansel's entry in the College Roll of Honour.*

Above: *El Alamein War Cemetery, Egypt.*

Overleaf: Daily Express *War Map of All Fronts, 1941.*

AP OF ALL FRONTS

REFERENCE

British Empire
Soviet Russia
Free French Empire, Belgian Congo and Dutch East Indies
Countries in Allied Military Occupation

Germany
Italian Empire
Axis Partners and Countries in Axis Military Occupation
Countries in Japanese Military Occupation
Pre-War Western Frontier of Soviet Russia

NAVAL BASES

	British		German
	Russian		Italian
	Dutch		Japanese
	American		French

Principal Railways
Principal Shipping Routes (Distances in Nautical Miles)
Cables   Oilfields
                  Oil-pipe Lines

British Consuls   American Consuls
Docks   Coaling Stations

Third Officer Claud Risley Hearn (Hampden B House 1932–33)

Lost at sea off the coast of Sierra Leone, on or about 27 October 1942, aged 24

Claud Hearn was born on 5 May 1918 in Wonersh, Surrey, to Frances (née Trotter), an army nurse, and Hugh Hearn, a lieutenant-colonel in the Royal Artillery.

On the outbreak of the Second World War Hearn joined the Merchant Navy. Serving with the Blue Funnel Line, he worked his way up the ranks to become a third officer. The Merchant Navy has historically been regarded as the less glamorous part of the naval effort during wartime, but was crucial to the survival of Britain, an island nation that has always required essential supplies from across the seas.

Hearn died on or about 27 October 1942 when his ship, the *Stentor*, homeward bound for Liverpool, was torpedoed off the coast of Freetown, Sierra Leone, by the German submarine *U-509*. He is commemorated at the Tower Hill Memorial in London, which remembers those lost at sea while serving in the Merchant Navy or in fishing fleets.

Lieutenant-Colonel Nigel Robert Mackie Skene, DSC RM (Durnford House 1920–25)

Killed in action while at sea on 15 November 1942, aged 35

Nigel Skene was born in Norwich on 2 March 1907 to Rev. Robert Skene, a Clerk in Holy Orders, and his wife Fanny (née Smith). At the College he became Head of House and a member of the Shooting VIII.

By 1930 Skene was in the RAF, and by 1931 he was flying torpedo bombers from the carrier HMS *Glorious*. In 1936 he transferred to the Royal Marines, and in 1940 was awarded the Distinguished Service Cross, 'Awarded for Air Operations', while assigned to another carrier, the *Ark Royal*. On 15 November 1942 he was on the HMS *Avenger*, an escort carrier protecting a convoy travelling from Gibraltar to the Clyde in Scotland, when it was hit by a torpedo from a German submarine commanded by Adolf Piening, a famous U-boat ace. The ship sank within two minutes; Skene was not among the survivors. He is commemorated at the Lee-on-Solent Fleet Air Arm Memorial in Hampshire.

Top: *Third Officer Claud Risley Hearn's entry in the College Roll of Honour.*

Above: *Lieutenant-Colonel Nigel Robert Mackie Skene, DSC.*

Fourth Officer Hubert Godfrey Harrison (Hampden House 1934–37)

Died in an accident in England on 7 December 1942, aged 22

Hubert Godfrey Harrison (always known as Godfrey) was born on 12 August 1920 in Maranoa, Brazil, to Sybil Harrison (née Hunt) and Hubert Harrison, a manager for the Booth Shipping Line. He was by all accounts a good-natured boy, who solved arguments over whose turn it was to do a family chore by simply doing it. Perhaps this was because he was a member of the College scout troop, or perhaps his innate helpfulness had made him join the scouts.

After school Godfrey went into broadly the same field as his father, becoming an apprentice officer in the New Zealand Line. In September 1939 Godfrey transferred to MV *Sussex*, which had to be towed back to Liverpool on her second voyage in late 1940, after suffering bomb damage. His last stint at sea was on the *Awatea*, a troopship, as fourth mate. The *Awatea* was torpedoed and sunk in the Mediterranean by a U-boat, but all personnel were rescued. Godfrey also survived the 21 hours of bombing endured by the rescuing ship, and was brought safely back to England on Survivor's Leave.

On 7 December 1942, Harrison joined friends at a Saturday night dance in Wimbledon, on the outskirts of London. He intended to catch the train home to Hampton Wick, where his family lived. However, in the blackout maintained to confuse enemy bombers, he miscounted the number of stops before he needed to alight, and got out of the train at Raynes Park Station, the next one along, by mistake. The side he exited on was next not to a platform but to a track, and Harrison was killed instantly when he was hit by a fast train.

Lieutenant John Christopher Langton, DSC and bar RN (Stenning and Hampden Houses 1926–28)

Killed when his boat was sunk off the coast of Algeria on 18 December 1942, aged 30

John was born on 22 June 1912 in a smart, newly built villa just off the seafront at Bexhill-on-Sea, to Herbert Langton, an army officer of large private means, and his wife Marie Antoinette (née Gehle), the daughter of a retired colonel.

After school John joined the P&O shipping line, and received training in the Royal Naval Reserve as part of his employment. Shortly before the war he was transferred to the Royal Navy as first lieutenant of HMS *Walker*, which guarded convoys against U-boats. Just ten days into the war the *Walker* collided with another destroyer, HMS *Vanquisher*, and Langton was ▶

Top: *Fourth Officer Hubert Godfrey Harrison.*

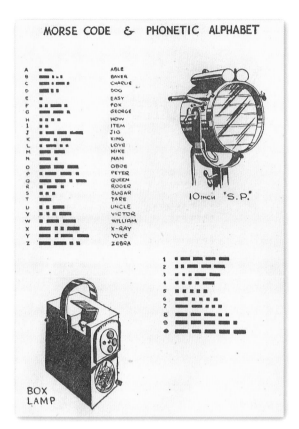

MORSE CODE & PHONETIC ALPHABET

A	▄ ▄▄▄	ABLE
B	▄▄▄ ▄ ▄ ▄	BAKER
C	▄▄▄ ▄ ▄▄▄ ▄	CHARLIE
D	▄▄▄ ▄ ▄	DOG
E	▄	EASY
F	▄ ▄ ▄▄▄ ▄	FOX
G	▄▄▄ ▄▄▄ ▄	GEORGE
H	▄ ▄ ▄ ▄	HOW
I	▄ ▄	ITEM
J	▄ ▄▄▄ ▄▄▄ ▄▄▄	JIG
K	▄▄▄ ▄ ▄▄▄	KING
L	▄ ▄▄▄ ▄ ▄	LOVE
M	▄▄▄ ▄▄▄	MIKE
N	▄▄▄ ▄	NAN
O	▄▄▄ ▄▄▄ ▄▄▄	OBOE
P	▄ ▄▄▄ ▄▄▄ ▄	PETER
Q	▄▄▄ ▄▄▄ ▄ ▄▄▄	QUEEN
R	▄ ▄▄▄ ▄	ROGER
S	▄ ▄ ▄	SUGAR
T	▄▄▄	TARE
U	▄ ▄ ▄▄▄	UNCLE
V	▄ ▄ ▄ ▄▄▄	VICTOR
W	▄ ▄▄▄ ▄▄▄	WILLIAM
X	▄▄▄ ▄ ▄ ▄▄▄	X-RAY
Y	▄▄▄ ▄ ▄▄▄ ▄▄▄	YOKE
Z	▄▄▄ ▄▄▄ ▄ ▄	ZEBRA

10 INCH 'S.P.'

1	▄ ▄▄▄ ▄▄▄ ▄▄▄ ▄▄▄
2	▄ ▄ ▄▄▄ ▄▄▄ ▄▄▄
3	▄ ▄ ▄ ▄▄▄ ▄▄▄
4	▄ ▄ ▄ ▄ ▄▄▄
5	▄ ▄ ▄ ▄ ▄
6	▄▄▄ ▄ ▄ ▄ ▄
7	▄▄▄ ▄▄▄ ▄ ▄ ▄
8	▄▄▄ ▄▄▄ ▄▄▄ ▄ ▄
9	▄▄▄ ▄▄▄ ▄▄▄ ▄▄▄ ▄
0	▄▄▄ ▄▄▄ ▄▄▄ ▄▄▄ ▄▄▄

BOX LAMP

compelled to shoot a man who had been trapped in the wreckage, to save him from further suffering in his last minutes.

In 1941 he came under the command of Captain Donald Macintyre, the legendary destroyer commander, whose reputation was summed up well in his post-war memoir, *U-boat Killer*. The team sank U-boats commanded by two of the most famous of all U-boat commanders, Günther Prien and Otto Kretschmer. The latter survived after tapping out the message 'We are sunking [sic]' in Morse code, which prompted the *Walker* to scour the waters for the U-boat crew, whom they managed to save. Kretschmer had spent eight months studying English before the war, staying at the house of a professor at Exeter University, though evidently he had not been a brilliant student. Langton gave them all whisky after they boarded, to stave off pneumonia.

In early 1942 he was transferred to HMS *Partridge*, another destroyer, based in the Mediterranean. He had already earned the Distinguished Service Cross for his 'successful enterprises against enemy submarines', as a *Manchester Evening News* report put it but now earned a bar to his DSC for conduct during Operation *Harpoon*, the despatch of a convoy to supply the British naval base at Malta. Later that year the ship was on an anti-submarine sweep in the Mediterranean when she was hit by a torpedo from a U-boat. The *Partridge* sank, and Langton perished with her. He is commemorated at the Chatham Naval Memorial.

Top: A Seaman's Pocket-Book, *page on Morse Code, June 1943.*

Above: *c1925–27 Stenning House photograph.*

Retired Captain Herbert Benjamin Whitelock Maling (Junior School and School House 1895–98)

Taken ill and died on active service in Turkey on 24 December 1942, aged 59

The war service of Retired Captain Herbert Maling, the oldest Old Brightonian to die on active service during the war, is perhaps the most mysterious of any of those commemorated in this book.

Herbert was born on 30 December 1882 in Speldhurst, Kent, to Irwin Maling and his wife Emily (née Whitelock). His was initially a conventional military career. A few years after leaving the College, where he participated in the Second XI as 'a clever player' according to a contemporary account in the April 1898 *Brighton College Magazine*, Maling fought with the East Surrey Regiment in the Boer War, and was mentioned in despatches. Staying in the army after the war, he served in the Somaliland operations of 1908–10.

In the Great War, Maling was transferred to the Connaught Rangers and came ashore with his battalion at Anzac Cove, Gallipoli, in Turkey, on 5 August 1915. During this campaign, it was in the Battle of Hill 60 on 21 August that the battalion suffered its greatest losses. According to an account of the battle by historian Bryan Cooper in his 1916 *The Tenth (Irish) Division in Gallipoli*:

> The Adjutant of the Rangers, Captain Maling, an officer to whose judgment and courage the battalion owed an incalculable debt, was severely wounded here.

Maling was again mentioned in despatches for his conduct in the Gallipoli campaign, and saw no further action. He retired from the army in 1924.

When the Second World War came Maling was recruited as a King's Messenger. The office, which dates back to the 15th century, involves conveying sensitive information and messages on behalf of the Crown, often to other nations. It was in this capacity that Maling found himself in Turkey in 1942 – sent there perhaps because he had been in the country during the Great War. We do not know why the government should have wanted to send a King's Messenger there in the first place, but we do know that Turkey was courted by both sides during the war. According to official records he died on Christmas Eve after being taken ill.

Above: *Retired Captain Herbert Benjamin Whitelock Maling.*

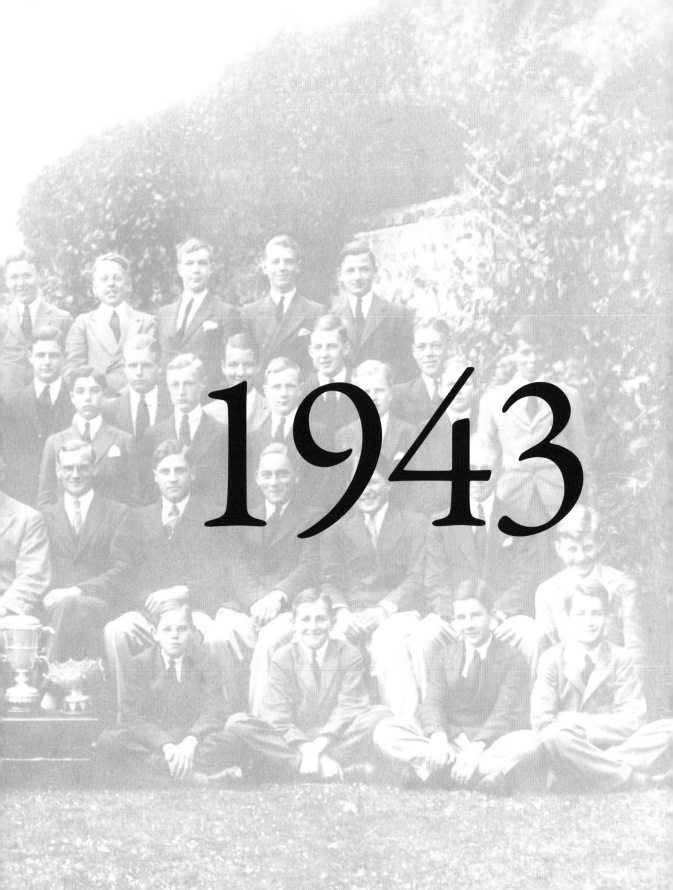

1943

Wilson's House, 1928.

Flight Lieutenant Douglas Herbert Scott Lonsdale, DFC RAFVR (Bristol House 1926–29)

Killed when his aircraft was shot down over the Netherlands on 3 January 1943, aged 31

Douglas was born on 4 October 1911 in Westham, Sussex, to Herbert Lonsdale and his wife Ethel (née Hallewell). At Brighton College he was both a House Prefect and a member of the Shooting VIII from 1927 to 1929, on the same team as Edward Young (see page 164).

During the war Lonsdale was in 9 Squadron of the RAF, flying bombers. In 1942 he was awarded the Distinguished Flying Cross. The citation included the lines:

As a captain of aircraft he takes meticulous care in the preparation of his sorties and performs them with vigour and determination. On several occasions he has spent long periods over heavily defended areas until able to identify his target clearly and bomb it from a low altitude.

On 3 January 1943 Lonsdale took part in a mission to bomb the German city of Essen. He crashed on the outskirts of Arnhem, in the Netherlands, after being attacked by a German plane. Lonsdale is buried at the Rheden (Heiderust) General Cemetery. He left a widow, Patricia.

Pilot Officer John Michael Whitehead RAAF (School House 1928–31)

Killed in a plane crash in Australia on 28 January 1943, aged 29

John was born in Bradford, Yorkshire, on 12 January 1914 to William Whitehead, a worsted spinner, and his wife Lucy (née Speight). At the College he appeared as one of General Stanley's daughters in Gilbert and Sullivan's *The Pirates of Penzance*, alongside Rhys Price, Kenneth Seth-Smith and Raymond Elliott (see pages 128, 95, and 38).

At some point after leaving the College he must have emigrated to Australia, because the next we hear of him is his death while serving in an Operational Training unit of the Royal Australian Air Force in Bairnsdale, Victoria. This was presumably in an aircraft accident, probably while training, though it is also possible that he was an instructor. He is buried in the Bairnsdale War Cemetery, Australia.

Top: *Flight Lieutenant Douglas Herbert Scott Lonsdale, DFC.*

Above: *Pilot Officer John Michael Whitehead.*

Flight Lieutenant Owen Cecil Chave RAFVR (Chichester House 1926–31)

Killed when his plane was shot down over Belgium on 14 February 1943, aged 30

Owen Chave was born on 29 April 1912, the son of Lady Rachel Chave (née Morgan) and Sir Benjamin Chave, a merchant seaman knighted for 'outstanding courage and leadership' during the Great War after his ship was torpedoed and sunk; Sir Benjamin is commemorated in the National Portrait Gallery.

Owen entered the College on the top classical scholarship and became both a Prefect and captain of the Shooting VIII. In adulthood he found it hard, as some very bright people do, to settle down. He worked first in insurance and then in teaching, while also dabbling in journalism, before going into commercial aviation.

Chave joined the RAF Reserve in 1936, and flew Stirling bombers in the war. He detailed his experiences in published poetry, both jocular and serious, including an excellent short poem, 'Night Bomber', that contrasted the glamour of Fighter Command with the undeserved lower profile of Bomber Command. A verse reads:

> Not theirs the sudden glow
> Of triumph that their fighter-brothers know;
> Only to fly through cloud, through storm, through Night
> Unerring, and to keep their purpose bright,
> Nor turn until, their dreadful duty done,
> Westward they climb to race the awakened sun.

On the night of 14 February 1943 his aircraft was shot down by a night-fighter over Belgium while on a bombing raid targeting the German city of Cologne. Chave and the rest of the crew are buried in the Heverlee Commonwealth War Cemetery.

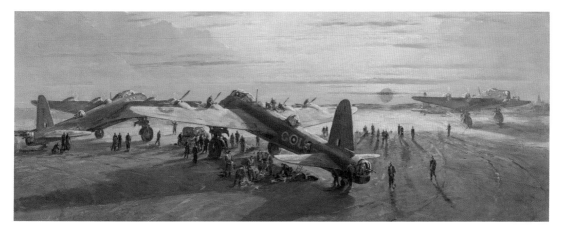

Top: *Flight Lieutenant Owen Cecil Chave.*

Above: Stirling Bomber Aircraft: Take-off at sunset, *by Charles Ernest Cundall, 1942.*

Lieutenant Michael Arthur Grant Allen, MC
(Bristol House 1934–37)

Died of wounds in Tunisia on 8 March 1943, aged 23

Michael Allen was born in Cubert, Cornwall, on 17 September 1919 to Arthur Allen, a British government official serving as Inspector for the Ministry of Communications in Egypt, and his wife Norah (née Byrne-Grant). Allen was a House Prefect, played for the 2nd XV, and competed for the Swimming VIII. He was also strong academically, receiving an 'A' in the School Certificate exam.

During the war Allen served in the Gordon Highlanders and then the 1st Battalion of the Black Watch. In 1942 he was posted to Egypt, where he took part in the victorious Second Battle of El Alamein. During this action he was wounded and awarded the Military Cross for bravery. The citation for the award included the lines:

> On the night of the 23/24 October 1942 South of Tel El Eisa this officer led his platoon successfully onto the final objective. During the advance he displayed great courage in the mêlées and hand-to-hand fighting which took place. Although wounded he continued to fight on, killing several of the enemy with his own bayonet and refusing to be pushed back until it was obvious that he could go on no longer.

Alan recuperated from his wounds until February 1943. By this time the Allies had pushed far to the west into Tunisia where, on 6 March, Axis forces launched a counter-attack against the British Army at the Battle of Medenine. The British managed to defend their position. However, their very success was instrumental in Allen's death: he took charge of some Italians who were surrendering, but as he approached the group one of them threw a grenade, seriously wounding him. Allen died the next day and is buried in Sfax Cemetery, Tunisia.

Lieutenant-Colonel Alfred James Frederick Sugden
(Durnford House 1916–20)

Died of wounds from friendly fire in India on 7 April 1943, aged 40

Alfred James Frederick Sugden was born on 18 August 1902 in the British Army garrison town of Rawalpindi in north-west India. His parents were Florence and Alfred Stanway Sugden, both members of the Army Educational Corps.

At Brighton College Alfred enjoyed success in athletics, before leaving in 1920 and entering the army's Royal Military Academy, Woolwich. After graduating from the Academy as an artillery

Above: *Lieutenant Michael Arthur Grant Allen, MC.*

specialist he was posted to Hong Kong, before returning to England, where he spent some time at the Staff College. While in England Sugden married Pamela Pickwoad, who bore him two daughters, Jenny and Rosemary. Sugden and his commanding officer outwitted the War Office, which had turned down a request for a postponement of his posting to India, submitted on the grounds that his wife was expecting their first child, by getting him onto an officer's gunnery course in England. This delayed his departure by enough time for him to see his newborn baby.

In 1938 Sugden finally went to India, where he was Master of the Bangalore Hounds. In the course of time he was placed in charge of the Indian Army's 160th Field Regiment Royal Artillery. Preparing for a new campaign, the regiment stepped up its live-firing exercises. Lieutenant-Colonel Sugden was critically injured by a stray shell during a practice artillery barrage, and died of his wounds two days later. He is buried in the Calcutta (Bhowanipore) Cemetery.

Major John Montague Peacock
(Wilson's House 1928–30)

Killed in action in Tunisia on 8 April 1943, aged 29

John was born on 13 April 1913 in Willesden, London, to Ethel May Peacock (née Firmin), a nurse, and Montague Peacock, an insurance clerk, who went on to serve as an airman in the Great War. In September 1939, the month that Britain entered the Second World War, he married Annabelle Pluck, who bore him a son, Michael, two years later.

Peacock fought with the 64th (Queen's Own Royal Glasgow Yeomanry) Anti-Tank Regiment. In 1942–43 the regiment supported the 78th Infantry Division of the Royal Artillery during Operation *Torch*, the Allied invasion of French North Africa. The regiment was sometimes referred to by battle-hardened soldiers as the 'Suicide Corps' because, as one former soldier explained, 'you had to be really close to the tanks for the firing to be effective'.

Peacock was killed in action on 8 April 1943. The date of his death and location of his grave, at the Medjez-El-Bab War Cemetery in Tunisia, suggest that he was killed during the 78th Division's assault on the Axis lines that helped to extinguish the enemy presence in North Africa in May 1943.

Top: *Lieutenant-Colonel Alfred James Frederick Sugden.*

Above: *Major John Montague Peacock.*

Sergeant Cedric Malaher Thompson
(Bristol House 1930–31)

Died on active service in North Africa on 26 April 1943, aged 27

Cedric Thompson was born in Bromley, Kent, on 3 February 1916, and was the only son of Gerald Thompson and his wife Hilda (née Malaher). He served in the RAF as a wireless operator and air gunner on bombers, and was killed on active service in April 1943. Thompson is buried at the Suez War Memorial Cemetery, on the western outskirts of the city. The date of his death, and location of his burial, suggest that he was killed in the closing stages of the Western Desert campaign, when the German and Italian troops were being defeated in Tunisia.

Captain Albert Frederick John Nethercott White
(Hampden House 1918–24)

Died on active service in New Guinea on 30 April 1943, aged 36

Albert was born in Dundalk, Ireland, to Frederick and Alice White on 4 November 1906. He served in the Australian Army, after enlisting in Brisbane. He died in April 1943 in New Guinea, a region subject to years of arduous warfare between the Allies and Japanese, while an acting captain with the New Guinea Force Air Liaison Group. We do not know if he was killed in combat, died in an accident, or succumbed to disease – many soldiers fell ill and died in the jungle. He left a widow, Edith, and is buried in the Port Moresby (Bomana) War Cemetery.

Top: *Sergeant Cedric Malaher Thompson.*

Above: *Captain Albert Frederick John Nethercott White.*

Sergeant Montagu Norminton Williams (Wilson's House 1925–28)

Died on active service in Wales on 29 May 1943, aged 32

Born on 21 April 1911 to Florian Williams and his wife Alfreda (née Schneider) of Hendon, Middlesex, Montagu rowed, ran and played rugby at the College. He served as an air gunner on bombers for the RAF during the war. He died on active service in Pembroke in May 1943. There was a nearby base at Pembroke Dock, equipped with the Short Sunderland flying boat. We cannot be certain he was stationed there, though we do know that he was not home on leave, as his family lived in Sutton, Surrey. His death notice in the newspaper referred to him touchingly as:

> Montagu Norminton (Tupp'ny) Williams, RAFVR, the adored husband of Beryl (née Gaul), of 6, Coniston Gardens, Sutton, Surrey, and darling Daddie [sic] of Michael and Felicity.

He is buried in All Saints Churchyard, Banstead, Surrey.

Top: *Australian soldiers disembark from aircraft at Wau to reinforce the advance on Salamaua, during the campaign in New Guinea, 1943.*

Above: *Grave of Sergeant Montagu Norminton Williams, Banstead (All Saints) Churchyard.*

Major Arthur Robert Checkley Barker
(Durnford House 1923–26)

Died in an accident in England on 5 June 1943, aged 34

Arthur Robert Checkley Barker was born on 29 March 1909 in Bristol, to Mabel and L. C. Barker, a railway engineer. In 1937 he married Sheila Parsons. Sheila was from Taunton, and the couple made their home there. In 1942 a son, Rodney, was born. During the war he served in the Royal Electrical and Mechanical Engineers, which maintains and repairs army equipment, where he was promoted to acting major.

On 5 June 1943 Barker died in an accident while on military service, probably in the district of Bodmin, Cornwall. We do not know precisely what happened, but the treeless landscape of Bodmin Moor would have been suitable for manoeuvres by the armoured vehicles on which Barker would probably have spent much of his time. Robert is buried in St Mary's Cemetery, Taunton.

Sub-Lieutenant Anthony Max Leslie Harris RN
(School House 1936–40)

Killed in a plane crash in the United States on 14 June 1943, aged 20

Anthony was born on 19 January 1923 in Brentford, Middlesex, to Arthur Harris and his wife Olga (née Hopkins). After Brighton College, where he was a House Prefect, editor of the *Brightonian* magazine, member of the Shakespeare Society, corporal in the OTC and member of the 1st XV, Harris joined the Royal Navy. There he served in the 1830 Naval Air Squadron, part of the Fleet Air Arm.

In 1943 the squadron was despatched to the United States to train in the Vought F4U Corsair fighter aircraft lent by the US to its ally. In June 1943 Harris was still in training when he crashed near the Old Stone Church Cemetery in Tiverton, Rhode Island. His plane exploded on impact and Harris was killed. He is buried in the Island Cemetery in Newport, Rhode Island.

Top: *Major Arthur Robert Checkley Barker.*

Above: *Sub-Lieutenant Anthony Max Leslie Harris.*

Flight Lieutenant Arthur Joseph Hyams RNZAF (Walpole House 1927–29)

Killed in a plane crash near Tutuba Island, in present-day Vanuatu, on 25 June 1943, aged 31

Arthur Hyams was born on 21 March 1912 to Elias Hyams, an importer and distributor, and Iris (née Mandel), of Wellington, New Zealand. He arrived at Brighton College in 1927.

Hyams enlisted in the Royal New Zealand Air Force in December 1939, after first writing to the Head Master, asking for a copy of his School Certificate, which he needed before applying. On 25 June 1943 Hyams was flying a Curtiss P-40 Kittyhawk fighter aircraft near Tutuba Island, Espiritu Santo, in the South Pacific. He requested permission to return and land as his instruments did not appear to be working properly. However, before he could reach the airstrip, the plane started to dive. An extract from the Court of Inquiry documents states:

The machine hit the water and exploded with a bright flash.

Three years earlier, in July 1940, Hyams had married Joan Ryan at Sacred Heart Basilica, Wellington. Their daughter, Robin, was born after his death. He is commemorated at the Bourail Memorial in New Caledonia.

Top: *Flight Lieutenant Arthur Joseph Hyams.*

Above: *Arthur Hyams, on the left, marries Joan Ryan, with bridal attendants in train, 1940.*

Private Dennis Cecil Clark (School House 1929–31)

Died in a prison camp in Thailand on 28 June 1943, aged 28

Dennis was born in Worthing on 2 October 1914 to Alice and John Clark. He joined Brighton College as a boarder in the Sixth Form. He was a member of the 1st XV and was described in the January 1932 issue of the *Brighton College Magazine* as:

> [having] improved, and is at times a really good player, though variable. He opens up the game well and has a strong cut through, but he must learn to collar low and with determination.

At some point after his time at the College, he appears to have emigrated to the Straits Settlements, a group of British colonies in south-east Asia, now largely in Malaysia, since he joined the Straits Settlement Volunteer Force fighting in Singapore.

Clark was captured on the fall of Singapore to the Japanese in February 1942, and enlisted as forced labour to build the Thai–Burma Railway, known as 'The Death Railway', living on meagre rations. He died of unknown causes in Thailand on 28 June 1943, and is buried in the Kanchanaburi War Cemetery in Thailand.

Flying Officer Christopher Posford Martin Phillips RAFVR (Chichester House 1936–40)

Died on active service in Tunisia on 12 July 1943, aged 20

Christopher was born in Steyning, Sussex, on 27 July 1922 to Cecil Phillips, a schoolmaster who became head of a prep school in Brighton, and his wife Mary (née Posford). At the College he was a School Prefect, and a member of both the 1st XV and Boxing VIII.

On leaving school he joined the RAF and flew bombers with 14 Squadron, which supported troops in East Africa and then in the Western Desert campaign. By July 1943 the squadron was sweeping the Mediterranean looking for submarines, flying the US Martin Marauder.

Christopher is buried in the Medjez-el-Bab War Cemetery in Tunisia, so we can surmise that he died there. The squadron was not based in Tunisia, so he is unlikely to have succumbed to illness. It is most likely that he crashed, either in an accident or because his plane was damaged during a mission.

Top: *Private Dennis Cecil Clark.*

Above: *Flying Officer Christopher Posford Martin Phillips.*

Lieutenant John David Brydges (Common Room 1939)

Died on active service in Italy on 16 July 1943, aged 28

John was born on 19 April 1915 into an educated and well-heeled family: his father, Edward Brydges, was a barrister, and his mother, Edith (née Cooper), an Oxford graduate at a time when proportionately many fewer women were granted degrees than are today.

He joined the College to teach Classics, which he had studied at Wadham College, Oxford, earning a First – a much rarer feat in those days. Brydges was a useful man to have on the staff, since he played rugby and cricket and was a keen musician. He was the leader of the chorus in the Aeschylus play *Agamemnon*, a tragedy in which the commander of the Greek forces at Troy is murdered by his wife after returning from the war.

Brydges did not return from war. He served with the 1/7th Battalion of the Middlesex Regiment, and died during the victorious Allied campaign to liberate Sicily, in July 1943. Brydges is commemorated at the Cassino Memorial on the mainland of Italy.

Warrant Officer Ian Wallace-Cox (Chichester 1935–37)

Killed in a plane crash in England on 27 July 1943, aged 22

Ian was born on 6 September 1920 in Upton-upon-Severn, Worcestershire, to Gordon Wallace-Cox and his wife Alice (née Shields). He was at Brighton College from 1935 to 1937, playing in the 1st XI and the 1st XV, and becoming a Prefect in his last year.

During the war he flew in the Armstrong Whitworth Whitley bomber, acting as bomb aimer and navigator. On 27 July 1943 he was in an aircraft that took off from Darley Moor Airfield in Derbyshire just after midnight. The aircraft was barely airborne when a flame trap on the port engine failed, causing the engine to catch fire. The aircraft quickly lost what little height it had and crashed in a field less than half a mile from the end of the runway, killing the whole crew. Wallace-Cox is buried in nearby Ashbourne Cemetery, but the natural world has also created its own memorial: a depression in the grass, created by the plane's impact, can still be seen in the field. He left a widow, Margery.

Top: *Lieutenant John David Brydges.*

Above: *Warrant Officer Ian Wallace-Cox.*

Sergeant John Frederick Alfred Trehearn
(Hampden B House, later Leconfield House 1936–40)

Killed in action over Germany on 30 July 1943, aged 21

John Trehearn was born on 21 May 1922 in Steyning, Sussex, to John Griffiths Trehearn of Durban, South Africa, and his wife Marian (née Williams). At the College he was a member of the Shooting VIII.

After school he joined the RAF, one of many South Africans who served with the RAF during the war, whose number included Pat Pattle, the man widely regarded as the highest scoring air ace in the RAF. During the war he served with 102 Squadron as a wireless operator and gunner in bombers, flying night raids over Germany. It was during one of these missions that Trehearn was killed on 30 July 1943, while flying in a Handley Page Halifax. Trehearn is buried in Ohlsdorf Cemetery in Hamburg.

Flight Lieutenant Derek George Leader-Williams
RAFVR (Chichester House 1928–33)

Killed in action in Germany on 6 September 1943, aged 28

Derek was born on 6 October 1914 in India, to Ernest Leader-Williams – a descendant of Sir Edward Leader-Williams, the Victorian engineering hero who designed the Manchester Ship Canal – and his wife Marguerite (née Vigers). He was a School Prefect at the College, and won a prize for French.

On the outbreak of war Leader-Williams enlisted in the RAF and was attached to 12 Squadron, a bomber unit based at RAF Downham Market in Norfolk. In September 1943 Leader-Williams and his rear gunner and close friend, Sergeant John Harding, were killed when their plane was shot down during a mission over Germany, although the remaining five crew members bailed out safely. He is buried in the Durnbach War Cemetery, south of Munich.

Top: Grave of Sergeant John Frederick Alfred Trehearn, Hamburg Cemetery, Germany.

Above: Flight Lieutenant Derek George Leader-Williams.

Lieutenant Peter Francis Hugh Wray RM (Chichester House 1936–39)

Killed in action in Italy on 17 September 1943, aged 22

Peter Wray was born in Brentford, Middlesex, on 2 March 1921 to Lesley Wray and his wife Marjorie (née Barnett). At the College he was in the 1st XV and declared *victor ludorum*, a title given to the best athlete on Sports Day.

When war began he was working at Fairmile Engineering, an innovative boat design company specialising in motor, gun and torpedo boats for the Admiralty. Wray would doubtless have been in a reserved occupation – not compelled to enlist because his civilian work was important to the war effort – but in 1941 he signed up for the Royal Marines. The following year he joined 41st Royal Marine Commando. In 1943 his unit took part in the assault on Sicily. Wray distinguished himself in this operation and was mentioned in despatches.

On 9 September 1943 the Allies invaded mainland Italy, landing at Salerno. Initially, the commandos were unopposed, but were then hit by a strong German counter-attack. On 17 September, the day before the Germans retreated, leaving Salerno to the Allies, Wray was killed during, or died from his wounds after, action on the hills by the village of Piegolelle. He is buried in the Salerno War Cemetery.

Martin Baxter-Phillips (Chichester House 1928–34)

Died of fever while a prisoner of war in Burma on 19 September 1943, aged 28

Martin was born on 12 June 1915 to Richard Baxter-Phillips, a schoolmaster, and his wife Katharine (née Winkworth), who lived in Cuckfield, Sussex. He had a distinguished time at the College, rising to be Head of House.

During the war he served in the Federated Malay States Volunteer Force, and was captured in the fall of Singapore to the Japanese in February 1942. He was set to work on a rubber plantation, where he fell sick and died on 19 September 1943. He is buried at the Thanbyuzayat War Cemetery in present-day Myanmar.

After the fall of Singapore we were both sent to Japanese work camps, and in May, 1943, to Siam, to work on the ill-fated Bangkok-Moulmein railway. Martin did a splendid job of work during the march from the base camp. He was then very fit, and shouldered additional packs, and gave a helping hand to many unfortunate fellows who were falling out by the way. We met again towards the end of August, at Tambaya Convalescent (so-called) Camp in Burma. Martin was not feeling too fit then; he had had malaria, and was still suffering from dysentery. But he was always cheerful and we met occasionally and had a chat. Early in September he developed cardiac beri-beri, and after about a fortnight he collapsed and died. The strain on the heart had been too great, and he passed away very quietly in the end. The body was cremated and the ashes buried in a little cemetery near the railway which we built.

Top: *Lieutenant Peter Francis Hugh Wray.*

Above: *Martin Baxter-Phillips, in the 1933 Prefects photograph.*

Above, right: *A friend of Martin Baxter-Phillips relates his death in the March 1946 issue of the* Brightonian.

Private John Bernard Langton
(Durnford House 1935–39)

Killed in action in Italy on
23 September 1943, aged 22

John Langton was born on 1 August 1921 to George Langton and his wife Margery (née Blunt) of Guildford, Surrey. After leaving the College in 1939 he joined the Queen's Westminsters as a Territorial Army reservist. Midway through the war, he was transferred to the 2nd Battalion of the King's Own Yorkshire Light Infantry. On 9 September 1943 his battalion took part in Operation *Avalanche*, a landing in the Gulf of Salerno, some 30 miles south of Naples. The aim was for troops to link up with the Allied forces that had conquered Sicily and moved onto the mainland. By 17 September the Allies had prevailed, and the Germans retreated from the beaches. However, frequent clashes with the enemy continued, and it was in this fighting that Langton was killed.

In his letter to the Head Master, Walter Hett, informing the school of the death, George Langton wrote that his son's letters 'were always cheerful', even though he 'never liked soldiering'. George Langton hoped to 'hear from someone with the battalion one day'. He and his wife did indeed hear from John's commanding officer, Captain Woodage, who described the private's death and burial:

On the morning of the 23rd, the company had to take a bridge strongly held by enemy M.G.s [machine guns]. I took six men, including your son, to clear a house on our right, which had been giving us a great deal of trouble. I regret to say that your son was killed by M.G. fire during this operation. I was within three yards of him at the time. It may be some consolation for you to know that his death was instantaneous and that he could have suffered no pain.

Langton's grave is in the Salerno War Cemetery.

Top: *Private John Bernard Langton.*

Above: *Men of the 9th Battalion, Royal Fusiliers at an observation post at the window of a ruined house, during Operation* Avalanche, *9 September 1943.*

Sergeant William Frank Reginald Allen Baillie
(Durnford House 1937–39)

Killed when his plane was shot down over Italy on 15 October 1943, aged 19

William, known as Bill, the son of Rex Baillie and his wife Marguerite, was born into a white colonial family in Kenya on 7 January 1924. On turning 18 he joined the RAF, and was assigned to 223 Squadron, flying bombers as an air gunner. He was stationed first in the Middle East and then in Italy, where his Martin Baltimore was hit by anti-aircraft fire, killing him and a fellow crew member; two others survived to become prisoners of war. In a long and moving letter to Walter Hett, his mother said:

> It has been a terrible shock to us. As you know he was my only child... He had so much to come back to and everybody loved him here as he was always so cheery and loved life so. How I pray this ghastly war will end this year.

Near the close of the letter she concluded:

> I think the people in England have been simply magnificent, but they must be very war weary. How wonderful old Churchill is.

Captain Raymon Arthur Lacoste
(Durnford House 1927–31)

Died on active service in Italy on 20 October 1943, aged 29

Raymon was born in Eastbourne on 19 March 1914 to Auguste Lacoste and his wife Lily (née O'Hara). During the war he served as a captain in the 113th Field Regiment of the Royal Artillery. He died on active service on the Italian mainland, only a month after it had been invaded by the Allies, and is buried at the Minturno War Cemetery, some 50 miles north of Naples. He left a widow, Isabel.

Top: *Sergeant William Frank Reginald Allen Baillie.*

Above: *Captain Raymon Arthur Lacoste.*

Battle for Italy, 1943–45

Troops dashing ashore during the invasion of Sicily, 10 July 1943.

Monte Camino, 1943. Stretcher-bearers bring casualties down the rain-swept mountain.

Invasion of Italian mainland at Salerno, 9 September 1943.

British and Polish troops raising the Union flag alongside the Polish flag in the ruins of the Monte Cassino Monastery, 18 May 1944.

Churchill tanks of 51st Royal Tank Regiment moving across the Italian countryside, July 1944.

Italian civilians clamber aboard a turretless Stuart tank as the 8th Army enters Arezzo, 15 July 1944.

A 5.5-inch gun of 178th Medium Regiment in action next to the Gothic Line, 24 December 1944.

British soldiers rest by an orchard wall during the Italian Campaign, 1943, *by Edward Jeffrey Irving.*

Wing Commander Richard Geoffrey England, DSO, DFC AAF (Gordon House 1930–33)

Killed in action on 22 October 1943 in the Netherlands, aged 27

Richard was born in Cardiff on 7 April 1916 to Richard Travell England and his wife Gwendoline (née Whitelaw). After leaving the College in 1933 he joined the Royal Artillery Air Force, which maintained a reserve of skilled part-time volunteers who could be deployed effectively in time of war.

When war came England served with 107 Squadron, flying bombing raids. On 9 November 1943 the Air Ministry announced that Acting Wing Commander England, who already had the Distinguished Flying Cross, had been awarded the Distinguished Service Order. The citation praised his 'inspiring leadership, great courage and exceptional skill'. By the time of this announcement, England had already been dead for 18 days, killed in a raid on Kamperland in the Netherlands. He is buried at the nearby Vlissingen Noorderbegraafplaats.

Flying Officer John Dixon (Hampden House 1934–38)

Killed in action in the Aegean Sea on 29 October 1943, aged 22

John Dixon was born in India on 10 November 1920, the son of Captain George Dixon of the Indian Army and his wife Norah (née Luby). At the College he was a member of the Shooting VIII.

By 1943 he was a flying officer with 47 Squadron, based at El Adem in Libya, just south of Tobruk. He was flying Beaufighters, known as 'armed rovers', which were an upgrade of the earlier Bristol Blenheim, and bristling with cannons and weaponry. Their role was to undertake anti-shipping sweeps across the Mediterranean. By late October, they were attacking German shipping sailing out of Greece and destined for Italy.

John and his navigator, Flying Officer George Terry, were unlucky to be shot down and killed on 29 October. The plane that caught them was a slow Arado 196 seaplane – much slower than the Beaufighter. It must have swooped down on them while they were attacking the ships, because Dixon fired his torpedoes before he was shot down. Dixon's name is listed on the Alamein Memorial in Egypt.

Top: Flushing (Vlissingen) Northern Cemetery, the Netherlands.

Above: John Dixon in the 1938 OTC shooting photograph.

Flight Sergeant John Victor Beverley Homewood (Hampden House 1936–38)

Died on active service in England on 29 October 1943, aged 22

John Homewood was born on 21 August 1921 to Gilbert Homewood, an art expert and assessor who resided in Hove. During the war he served in the RAF, flying the Hurricane fighter bomber from RAF Ayr. He died on active service on 29 October 1943, and is buried in the Western Road Cemetery at Haywards Heath, West Sussex. Given his burial in England, and the fact that the date of his death did not coincide with any major bombing raids, it is likely that he was killed in an accident.

Major William Hay Purves, MBE (Chichester House 1925–29)

Died on active service in the Middle East on 18 November 1943, aged 32

Born in Burnley on 19 July 1911 to William James Purves and his wife Lily (née Smith), William Hay Purves became Head of House at the College, while also playing for the 1st XV. Perhaps appropriately for a boy of such exalted status at the school, he played a Noble Lord in a production of Gilbert and Sullivan's *The Mikado*.

During the war he served in the Middle East with the Royal Army Medical Corps, and won the MBE for gallantry on 18 February 1943, when his unit would almost certainly have been supporting troops fighting the German and Italian forces in Tunisia.

The circumstances surrounding his death are mysterious. By November 1943 the British Army's front line in the Mediterranean had shifted from the Middle East to Italy, but he is recorded as dying in the Middle East, and is buried in the Fayid War Cemetery in Egypt. It is possible that he died of wounds received earlier, or of a disease. He left a widow, Constance, a fellow medic.

Top: *Flight Sergeant John Victor Beverley Homewood.*

Above: *Major William Hay Purves, MBE.*

Lieutenant Alan Willoughby Toley
(Wilson's and Chichester Houses 1931–36)

Killed in a plane crash in Greece on 1 December 1943, aged 25

Alan, the son of Ernest Toley and his wife Ethel (née Lawrence), was born on 13 December 1917 in Middlesex. At the College he was Head of House and captained the 1st XV, where he was judged as 'a very fair' skipper, with 'very sound' defence. During the war he became a lieutenant in the Royal Tank Regiment, fighting in the Middle East. He then joined Force 133 of the Special Operations Executive, charged with diverting German forces from the defence of France by tricking them into believing there was a planned invasion of Greece. William Phillips (see page 128) was in the same unit. Alan was killed in an air crash in Greece, and is buried at the Phaleron War Cemetery in Athens.

Major Tristan George Lance Ballance, MC
(Common Room 1937–40)

Killed in action in Italy on 4 December 1943, aged 27

Tristan, the son of Sir Hamilton Ballance, an eminent surgeon, and his wife Lady Mercy (née Barrett), was born in Norwich on 21 April 1916. After being educated at Uppingham School and Brasenose College, Oxford, he joined Brighton College as a master, while continuing to play county cricket for Norfolk, as a strong batsman and excellent bowler. Ballance was a member of the school choir while he was a member of staff at the College and

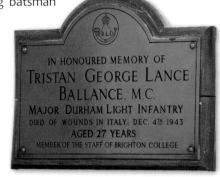

was involved in many of the school's drama productions, including *Ruddigore* and *Trial by Jury*.

In 1940 he joined the 16th Battalion of the Durham Light Infantry, fighting in North Africa, where he won the

Top: *Lieutenant Alan Willoughby Toley.*

Above, left: *Major Tristan George Lance Ballance, MC.*

Above, right: *Major Tristan George Lance Ballance's memorial plaque in the Brighton College Chapel.*

Military Cross in 1943 – becoming a real war hero four years after playing a war hero, Captain Dallas, VC, in *Shivering Shocks*, a play for boys performed at the College. His citation read:

> By his leadership and example, he was able to keep his men firing and the enemy in check until all his ammunition was exhausted.

In September 1943 the Allies invaded the Italian mainland, and Ballance, known by his comrades as George, coped with his usual good humour. A letter to his sister from the front, both touching and amusing, records his sympathy for the plight of the deprived Italian populace and his regret at not receiving earlier letters from her. His comical explanation:

> The other letters you speak of will probably catch me up in due course, but mail has been very bad recently. I think the weather has had something to do with it. We had notification the other day of a certain amount of outgoing mail that had got rain-sodden. I think the postman's tent blew away, so that was the end of that one.

On 4 December he was killed in an attack on the heavily fortified Gustav Line and is buried at the Minturno War Cemetery.

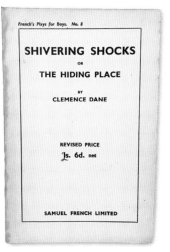

Pilot Officer Richard Anthony Bayldon (Hampden House 1937–40)

Killed in action over Germany on 16 December 1943, aged 20

Born on 7 August 1923 to Captain Richard Bayldon and his wife Claudine (née Dampney) of Barnstaple, Devon, Richard junior was in the Tennis VI at school.

During the war he flew bombers for 9 Squadron, which was stationed at RAF Bardney in Lincolnshire. In December 1943 he was flying his Avro Lancaster bomber on a mission over Berlin when his plane came down, presumably hit by either an enemy fighter or anti-aircraft fire. He is buried in the Berlin 1939–45 War Cemetery in Charlottenburg, the site of Frederick the Great's palace.

Top: *French's Acting Edition of* Shivering Shocks, *by Clemence Dane.*

Above: *Pilot Officer Richard Anthony Bayldon's entry in the College Roll of Honour.*

1944

1933 OTC shooting team photograph. Eliot Welchman (see page 143) is on the bottom row, on the left.

Lieutenant Rhys Alfred Price (School House 1928–30)

Killed by a German bomb in England on 5 January 1944, aged 29

Rhys was born on 6 March 1914 to Ernest Price and his wife Beatrice (née Pawley). At the College he established a niche playing female parts in Gilbert and Sullivan operettas, as a schoolfellow of Yum Yum in *The Mikado*, a daughter of General Stanley in *The Pirates of Penzance*, and Dame Carruthers, housekeeper of the Tower, in *The Yeomen of the Guard*.

During the war he served with the Royal Artillery, initially in India and then back in England – he was probably disqualified from front-line duties because of his poor eyesight. In January 1944 Price was stationed as an anti-aircraft officer with the 131st Light Anti-Aircraft Regiment at St Leonards-on-Sea, near Hastings. While on duty he was killed by a bomb dropped from a German plane. He left a widow, Irene, and is buried at Hove Cemetery.

Captain William Ronald Phillips (Chichester House 1931–35)

Died while on special operations in Greece on 29 January 1944, aged 26

William was born on 13 June 1917 to Ernest Phillips, a coal merchant, and his wife Ursula (née Nunns), of Great Amwell, Hertfordshire. His grandfather on his father's side, also called William, was a well-known social reformer who embraced causes as diverse as Italian democracy, free education, environmental protection and bandstands in public parks.

After leaving the College, where he was a member of the Boxing VIII, William opted for a life of extraordinary adventure. In north-eastern Africa, he worked as a bodyguard to Haile Selassie when the Ethiopian Emperor returned to his country with British military support in 1941, ejecting the Italians, and served as a bimbashi (major) in the Sudan Defence Force. He later joined Force 133 of the Special Operations Executive, charged with diverting German forces from the defence of France ahead of the Allied invasion in June 1944 by fooling Hitler into believing in a planned invasion of Greece. He died on this mission in January 1944 in unknown circumstances, and is buried at the Phaleron War Cemetery.

Top: *Lieutenant Rhys Alfred Price.*

Above: *Captain William Ronald Phillips.*

Lieutenant Percy Godfrey Openshaw RN (School House 1926–28)

Died at sea off the coast of Italy on 18 February 1944, aged 31

Percy Godfrey Openshaw was born on 16 May 1912 in Lewisham, then in Kent, to Percy Austin Openshaw, a schoolmaster who later became a headmaster and priest, and Hilda (née Jarratt). In 1935 he became a lieutenant in the Royal Navy, and the next year married Ena Bayliss, who bore him two daughters, Angela and Jennifer. Shortly after his wedding he took part in the evacuation of refugees from the Spanish Civil War.

During the Second World War he was aboard the battleship HMS *Resolution* when she participated in the unsuccessful attempt to capture the Vichy French port of Dakar in French West Africa. The ship was torpedoed by the enemy French during the mission and was sent to the US for repair. Openshaw was reassigned to HMS *Pegasus*, a seaplane carrier escorting convoys. He was then assigned to HMS *Penelope*, a light cruiser serving in the Mediterranean, nicknamed HMS *Pepperpot* by her crew because of the number of holes left in her by enemy action.

On 18 February 1944 the *Penelope* was torpedoed and sunk by a German submarine off the coast of Anzio in Italy, where the Allied forces had the previous month established a bridgehead. Only one third of the crew survived, and Openshaw was not among them. He is commemorated at the Portsmouth Naval Memorial. In a poignant postscript, his grandson, Commodore James Godfrey Higham, is the commander of the Portsmouth base at the time of writing. Shortly after beginning his duties, he found the battle-worn ensign of the doomed HMS *Penelope* in a storeroom.

Top: *Lieutenant Percy Godfrey Openshaw.*

Above: *The port side of HMS* Penelope, *riddled by bomb splinters (hence its nickname HMS* Pepperpot*), with smiling members of the crew, during a visit by the Duke of Gloucester in April 1942.*

Lance Corporal Bruce Montague Spencer
(School House 1929–31)

Died on active service in Italy on 1 March 1944, aged 28

Born on 13 February 1916 in south-west London to Roland Spencer and his wife Eva, of Great Bentley, Essex, Bruce served with the Royal Fusiliers, an infantry regiment, during the war. He took part in the long and difficult fight up the Italian mainland by Allied forces, fighting at Salerno, where the Allies landed, and Monte Cassino. He was mentioned in despatches. In the winter of early 1944 the regiment took part in vicious skirmishes, despite the lack of a full-scale offensive. Spencer died on active service during this period, and is commemorated at the Cassino Memorial.

Flight Sergeant Oscar George Ackerman
(Bristol House 1927–31)

Died in an aircraft collision off Scotland on 5 March 1944, aged 31

Oscar Ackerman was born in Shanghai on 1 March 1913, the son of Gilbert Ackerman and his wife Amelia (née Novak), both from Wales. Gilbert was an accountant for the British American Tobacco Company. Tragically, Amelia died giving birth to Oscar and his twin sister Emilie. At the College he was a member of the Boxing VIII and a House Prefect, before following his father into the British American Tobacco Company and being posted to a factory in Hankou, a city on the River Yangtze.

During the war Ackerman was sent for RAF basic training to Blackpool, where he met and married his landlady's daughter, Barbara-Jean. In 1941 he was posted to Egypt, where he flew Wellington bombers. His crew undertook night raids over the Western Desert, targeting Panzer divisions and ports such as Benghazi to weaken Rommel's supply lines.

By July 1942, Ackerman had completed 30 operational missions – the quota for airmen before they were entitled to serve in a non-combat role for a period. As he stood on a warship in Alexandria waiting to depart, news came through of a major German offensive: the First Battle of El Alamein had begun. Ackerman was immediately recalled to Cairo and assigned to the crew of a Wellington in 104 Squadron. On their first mission, the aircraft was hit and caught fire. Ackerman and his crew

Top: *Lance Corporal Bruce Montague Spencer.*

Above: *Flight Sergeant Oscar George Ackerman.*

bailed out, but he was the only survivor. Landing behind enemy lines, he spent several days in the desert without food or water before he was found by Allied Special Forces. For this adventure he was enrolled in the Caterpillar Club, an award created by the Irvin Parachute Company for airmen surviving escape by parachute from a disabled plane.

In 1943 Ackerman was posted to RAF Cark in Cumbria, and was responsible for flying missions to train new wireless operators and air gunners. In one of his regular letters to Barbara-Jean, Oscar wrote about a flight planned for the next day. He was hoping it would be cancelled due to a poor weather forecast, but the mission went ahead. In stormy weather with poor visibility, Oscar's Anson collided with another training aircraft and ditched off the Mull of Galloway. This time there were no survivors. His son, also named Oscar George in memory of his father, was born six weeks later. The elder Oscar is buried in an Imperial War Graves Commission grave outside the old church in St Brides-super-Ely, Cardiff, where he had married just 16 months earlier.

Lieutenant-Colonel Rudolf Fitzroy Reginald Rouse, DSO (Junior School 1918, Hampden House 1920–24)

Killed in action in Burma on 11 March 1944, aged 37

The grandly named Rudolph Fitzroy Reginald Rouse was born on 15 February 1907 in India to Frederic Philip Pierrepoint Rouse and his wife Maud. His father served in the Supply and Transport Corps of the Indian Army, reaching the rank of captain, enabling Rudolf to win a Gill Scholarship to study at the College – this scholarship, funded by the family of William Gill, army officer, explorer, spy and Old Brightonian executed by hostile Bedouins in 1882, was open only to the sons of army officers. Rouse became a School Prefect and played for the 1st XV.

After leaving the College Rouse joined the British Army, serving in the Royal Artillery, before transferring to the Indian Army as a lieutenant in 1930. By the closing stages of the Second World War he was an acting lieutenant-colonel in the 2nd Punjab Regiment, and had been awarded the Distinguished Service Order. He was killed in action fighting the Japanese in Burma on 11 March 1944, leaving a widow, Hilda, and is buried in the Taukkyan War Cemetery.

Top: *Oscar Ackerman's membership card for the famous Caterpillar Club.*

Above: *Lieutenant-Colonel Rudolf Fitzroy Reginald Rouse, DSO.*

Lieutenant Dennis George Frank Peirce
(Hampden House 1932–35)

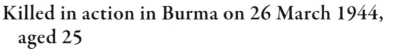

Killed in action in Burma on 26 March 1944, aged 25

Dennis Peirce was a local boy, born on 3 June 1918 in Brighton to Mabel and Richard Peirce, an architect and surveyor. He attended Brighton College for three years from 1932. In 1940 he married Joan, an auxiliary nurse. A son, Richard, was born in 1942.

In 1940 Peirce joined the Royal Sussex Regiment's new 9th Battalion, known as the Shiny Ninth, based in Britain. There was a severe shortage of military equipment because the army's British Expeditionary Force had left much of it behind when evacuated from Dunkirk, but a deal was done with the local RAF fighter station: six bottles of whisky were exchanged for 1,000 rounds of ammunition.

In October 1942 the Shiny Ninth departed Portsmouth for India. By March 1944 the 9th Battalion had entered Burma and advanced to Teknaf on the banks of the Naf River. It was given orders to cross the river and attack two tunnels, where the Japanese had constructed three forts. On 26 March the battalion's B Company launched its assault and reached its objective, the Western Tunnel. Soon it was under heavy attack from the Japanese, and there were many casualties. Lieutenant Peirce and his platoon tried, but failed, to climb the steep slope, so instead had to cross the entrance of the tunnel, which was covered by heavy enemy fire, to reach the top. During this attempt, Peirce and seven other men were killed, with one more later dying of his wounds. Lieutenant Peirce is buried in Taukkyan War Cemetery in Myanmar (Burma).

Flight Lieutenant John Gifford Stower RAFVR
(Hampden House 1932–33)

Shot for escaping from a prison camp in Germany on 31 March 1944, aged 27

John was born in Argentina on 17 September 1916 to Herbert Stower and his wife Euphemia (née Moffat), known as Effie, two Britons who had emigrated to the country. He flew bombers during the war, and was shot down while serving with 140 Squadron and taken prisoner. In 1943 he escaped the Stalag Luft III prison camp in what was then Germany, but is now part of Poland, but was recaptured after a few days.

Top: *Lieutenant Dennis George Frank Peirce.*

Above: *Flight Lieutenant John Gifford Stower.*

Sonderausgabe

zum
Deutschen Kriminalpolizeiblatt

Herausgegeben vom Reichskriminalpolizeiamt in Berlin

Erscheint nach Bedarf	Zu beziehen durch die Geschäftsstelle Berlin C 2, Werderscher Markt 5—6

16. Jahrgang	Berlin, den 16. Juni 1943	Nummer 4610

Nur für deutsche Behörden bestimmt!
Die Sonderausgaben sind nach ihrer Auswertung sorgfältig zu sammeln und unter Verschluß zu halten.

A. Neuausschreibungen.

Entwichene kriegsgefangene Offiziere.

I. Flucht von britischen und amerikanischen Fliegeroffizieren aus dem Luftwaffenlager 3 in Sagan (Schlesien).

Von den aus dem Luftwaffenlager 3 in Sagan (Schlesien) entwichenen 26 britischen und amerikanischen Fliegeroffizieren sind **noch flüchtig:**
Hill, William, Ltn., 21. 9. 15 ?, Gef.-Nr. 1369 Stalag Luft 3;
Morison, Walter, Hptm., 26. 11. 19 London, Gef.-Nr. 476/Stalag Luft 3;

Stower, John Gifford, Obltn., 15. 9. 16 Ingenio La Esperanza (Argentinien), Gef.-Nr. 836/Stalag Luft 3;
Welch, Patrick, Obltn., 12. 8. 16 Dorset, Gef.-Nr. 610/Stalag Luft 3.
Morison, Stower und Welch sind hierunter abgebildet.
Weitere energische Fahndung! Festnahme!

16. 6. 43. **KPLSt Breslau.**

Walter Morison

John Stower

Patrick Welch

Above: *A wanted poster issued by the Germans for three RAF officers – Patrick Welch, John Stower and Walter Morrison – after their escape from Stalag Luft III on 12 June 1943. Stower was recaptured but escaped a second time, only to be murdered by the Gestapo on 31 March 1944.*

In 1944 Stower took part in the famous Great Escape of 73 Allied prisoners from the camp, immortalised in the Hollywood film of the same name. Near the end of the film a large group of them are led into a field, where they are shot. Stower was one of those men, although in real life the prisoners were executed either singly or in pairs.

He is buried in the Poznan Old Garrison Cemetery, near the camp, and commemorated at a local memorial to the executed men. Margaret Dobson, John's aunt, told Walter Hett, the College Head Master, in a letter:

> It has been a great shock to us all to think that these fine fellows who have done so much for us should be shot in cold blood by the Germans.

Sergeant Lionel Edward John Baily (Chichester House 1937–40)

Killed in a plane crash off the coast of Italy on 22 May 1944, aged 21

Lionel Baily was born in Barnet, Middlesex, on 30 August 1922 to John Baily, a hardware merchant, and his wife Millicent (née Walby).

After three years at the College, where he won gold in an 880-yard race, Baily enlisted in the RAF in September 1940. He trained as a wireless operator and air gunner, and then in signals and air observation. In 1944 he was assigned to 18 Squadron, based at Marcianise airfield, about 17 miles north of Naples.

In the first five months of 1944 Lionel and his crew mainly flew missions to reconnoitre enemy road traffic in the area between Cassino, Anzio and Rome, operating the Boston III, a US aircraft designed as a light bomber and reconnaissance machine. On 22 May his plane took off shortly after midnight to conduct armed reconnaissance. The plane was reported to have flown into the sea, after the pilot struggled with poor visibility. Baily is remembered at the Malta Memorial, a monument to aircrew who lost their lives in the Mediterranean and have no known grave.

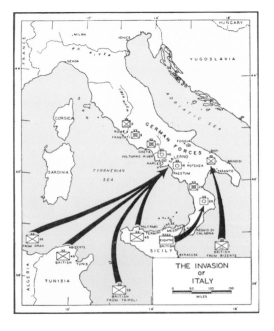

Top: *Sergeant Lionel Edward John Baily.*

Above: *Map of the Allied invasion of Italy, 1943.*

Captain Gilbert Harris Leny Buchanan
(Gordon House 1925–28)

Killed in action on 22 May 1944 in Italy, aged 34

Gilbert was born in Llandrindod Wells, Wales, on 10 April 1910 to Emily Buchanan (née Shannon) and Harris Buchanan, an elderly retired major who had fought in the Second Afghan War of 1878–80. His grandfather, Gilbert John Lane Buchanan, had been a general. After leaving Brighton College, where he played football, fives, and a fairy in Gilbert and Sullivan's *Iolanthe*, Buchanan did not choose the military as a career like his father and grandfather, but instead went into insurance.

During the Second World War he joined the 51st (Leeds Rifles) Royal Tank Regiment, which in 1940 guarded the Northumberland coast against the threat of German invasion. In 1943 the regiment distinguished itself by defending the line against a German counteroffensive in Tunisia. In April 1944 the regiment embarked for Naples. A month later it was supporting the Canadian infantry in an attack on Cassino, during which Buchanan was killed in action when a shell hit his tank. He is buried in the Cassino War Cemetery.

Lieutenant Sidney Stanley Fase
(School House 1935–36)

Died of wounds in Italy on 4 June 1944, aged 22

Sidney was born on 26 January 1922 in Lewisham, London, to Sidney Harold Fase, an engineer, and his wife Edith (née Stanley). At the College he played rugby and a little cricket, and performed in a school concert.

He joined the Royal Sussex Regiment in 1941, and fought with its 1st Battalion in the victorious campaign to capture Tunisia from the Axis powers. His battalion then moved on to Italy, where in February 1944 Fase was wounded during the battle to capture Monte Cassino, a key stronghold in the Germans' heavily fortified Winter Line. He died from these wounds on 4 June 1944, the day the Allies entered Rome, having circumvented the Winter Line after landing at Anzio earlier in the year. Fase is buried at the Sangro River War Cemetery in Italy.

Top: *Captain Gilbert Harris Leny Buchanan.*

Above: *Lieutenant Sidney Stanley Fase.*

Battle for Normandy, June to August 1944, through the eyes of four artists

Wounded British soldiers on Gold Beach during the D-Day landings, 6 June 1944, *by J. C. Heath.*

The Landing in Normandy; Arromanches, D-Day plus 20, 26 June 1944, *by Barnett Freedman.*

Bernard Law Montgomery, 1st Viscount Montgomery of Alamein, *by Frank Salisbury, 1945; the Field Marshal points to Normandy.*

A few British soldiers and some American Navy ratings sit on the deck of a US tank landing ship (LST). They sit casually, the foremost man reading a book. Other vessels can be seen at sea in the background.

Lieutenant Raymond 'Bunny' Charles Belcher (Chichester House 1937–41)

Killed in action in France on 6 June 1944, aged 20

Bunny was born in Abingdon, Oxfordshire, on 23 June 1923, to Bernard Belcher, a wine merchant and amateur dramatics enthusiast, and his wife Joyce (née Sides). He won a scholarship to Brighton College, but was also a good sportsman, earning a place in the 1st XV and playing tennis, squash and fives for the school.

On leaving the College he trained as an officer at Sandhurst, and, as the outstanding cadet of his troop, was presented with a special belt. He served with the Airborne Light Tank Squadron and then with the 6th Airborne Armoured Reconnaissance Regiment, an elite unit that required members to pass a special intelligence test and then train as parachutists. His instructor on this course described him as 'cheerful' and 'humerous [sic]'. By this time he had met Corporal Kay Pearce of the Auxiliary Territorial Service, the women's branch of the army. After a whirlwind romance, they married a month after they met.

With D-Day approaching, Bunny was placed in charge of the regiment's Harbour Party, a group of around 15 parachutists whose role was to jump with the very first units to land on French territory, reconnoitre, and secure strategically important points. His Short Stirling aircraft crashed on the night of D-Day, probably after being shot down, killing everyone on board.

As the plane had caught fire, detonating the shells and bullets and other explosives aboard, the crash site was deemed too dangerous for recovery of the bodies. It took many months for the Comte of the local château to persuade the Allies to arrange a military team to make it safe enough for the deceased to be removed.

The Belchers' only child, Anthony, was born on 9 September 1944, three months after his father's death. Bunny is buried at Ranville War Cemetery in France.

Top: *Lieutenant Raymond 'Bunny' Charles Belcher.*

Above: *King George VI inspects paratroops of the 6th Airborne Division, 16 March 1944.*

Lieutenant-Colonel Joseph Guest Holman (Walpole House 1920–24)

Lost at sea off France on 8 June 1944, aged 37

Joseph was born in Bristol on 24 March 1907 to Joseph Guest Holman, MC, MBE and his wife Beatrice (née Lane). As an avid fisherman, Holman made a good match in 1929 when he married Frederika, daughter of a fishing fleet owner. They had two children, Lynette and Roger. He qualified as a naval architect before the war, before briefly running a successful garage business and finally joining the family firm of grain merchants.

Despite his pre-war career, Holman opted for the army over the navy during the war, perhaps because his father had fought in that service, earning the MC. He served in the Royal Army Ordnance Corps, which kept the army supplied and repaired equipment.

On 8 June 1944, two days after D-Day, the Allied landings in Normandy, his unit, 17 Vehicle Company, was sent to France as part of a small advance force of reconnaissance units. His boat was torpedoed en route, and Holman, by this time a temporary lieutenant-colonel, was lost. He was posthumously mentioned in despatches. However, his family did not know this at the time. Anxious to piece together the exact details of his demise, his mother posted a notice in a newspaper announcing that he was 'missing at sea' and declaring: 'Any information gratefully received.' Holman is commemorated at the Bayeux Memorial in Normandy.

Trooper Edward Herbert Kenney (School House 1934–39)

Died of wounds in France on 8 June 1944, aged 23

Born in Chelsea on 11 May 1921 to Edward Herbert Kenney and his wife Olive (née Bellatti), Edward Herbert junior was a House Prefect and editor of the *Brightonian*, the College magazine. He went on to University College London (misleadingly named so at the time, since the college had been evacuated to Aberystwyth because of the war).

He joined the Life Guards, which took part in the Normandy landings of June 1944, serving as a trooper (the cavalry equivalent of a private). Trooper Kenney died of his wounds on only the third day of the campaign (not in July, as stated in the College Roll of Honour). After his death his father wrote to Walter Hett:

▶

Top: *Lieutenant-Colonel Joseph Guest Holman.*

Above: *Trooper Edward Herbert Kenney's entry in the College Roll of Honour.*

Our boy had some money saved, and my wife and I would like this to be presented to the College in memory of him.

In response, Hett suggested that it should be donated to the Centenary Endowment Fund, with a scholarship named after him. Kenney is buried in the Hermanville War Cemetery.

Captain Paul Gilbert Franklin (Durnford House 1927–30)

Killed in action in France on 14 June 1944, aged 31

Paul Franklin was born on 24 May 1913 to William Franklin, a commercial traveller, and his wife Julia (née Collard). At the College he fought in the Boxing VIII as a flyweight. A fellow team member was Oscar Ackerman (see page 130). He was a plucky fighter, as shown by one match report describing a fight against Epsom College:

Hewitt [his losing opponent] looked the older and more powerful, but Franklin by continual use of a good straight left gradually forced a most meritorious victory after receiving a good deal of punishment in the opening stages.

In 1941 Paul enlisted in the 3rd Regiment of the Royal Horse Artillery, which landed in Normandy soon after the Allied invasion in 1944. Only eight days after D-Day he was killed in Operation *Perch*, the battle to capture Caen during the hard fighting to break the Allies out of their small beachhead. He is buried in the Bayeux War Cemetery.

Top: *Captain Paul Gilbert Franklin.*

Above: *Paul Franklin in the 1929–30 Brighton College boxing team photograph, standing third from right. Stephen Donoghue (top row, far left) and Oscar Ackerman (middle row, second from left) (see pages 66 and 130) are also in the photo.*

Squadron Leader William Peter Jefferies RAFVR (Stenning House 1927–30)

Died on active service in England on 16 June 1944, aged 31

William was born on 14 May 1913 to William Peter Thierry Jefferies and his wife Winifred (née Fuidge), of Clifton, Bristol. He died while on active service near Chippenham in Wiltshire in June 1944. As he was a flying instructor we can surmise that he was probably based at nearby RAF Melksham, where aircrew were trained, and was probably killed while teaching an inexperienced pilot. This confirms how even RAF duties away from the front line could be dangerous. Jefferies is buried at Haycombe Cemetery in Bath.

Captain George Vivian Derek Russel (Walpole and School Houses 1931–35)

Died in an accident in England on 22 June 1944, aged 26

George was born in Thanet, Kent, on 20 April 1918, to Francis Russel, a veteran of the First World War who later became an estate agent, and his wife Adelina (née Elliott). At the College George was in the swimming team, and a corporal in the Officer Training Corps.

During the Second World War he served as a pilot in the Air Observation Post 661 Squadron. The pilots, who belonged to the army, looked for targets on the ground that could be attacked by artillery or aircraft, and directed their fire. In addition, they undertook reconnaissance, taking aerial photos. Their role was crucial in the 1944 reconquest of France, when the Allies were outnumbered by the Germans but still won, largely because of the intelligent use of superior airpower.

However, Russel was fated not to take part in this enterprise: a month before his squadron flew to Normandy, he was killed in an accident. This was probably a plane crash, given the large number of men who died in aircraft accidents during the war, though we do not know this for sure. He is buried in the St Peter and St Paul Churchyard in Cudham, Kent.

Top: *Squadron Leader William Peter Jefferies.*

Above: *Captain George Vivian Derek Russel.*

Flying Officer Gordon Fraser RAFVR (Wilson's House 1923–26)

Died on active service in France on 25 June 1944, aged 34

Born on 11 August 1909 to Robert Fraser and his wife May (née Gillespie), Gordon served with 102 Squadron during the war, flying bombers. By 1944 the unit was equipped with the Handley Page Halifax.

We can infer from his place of burial, Fontaine l'Étalon Churchyard in France's Pas-de-Calais province, that he was killed on a bombing mission. This was far from the Allied forces in Normandy, but Pas-de-Calais, the site of a V-2 flying bomb base and enemy troops, was bombed by the Allies all the same – not least because the Allies devised an elaborate deception that Pas-de-Calais would be the site of the main Allied invasion, and Hitler continued to believe this for some time even after the Allies landed in Normandy. Gordon left a widow, Angela, who may have been a cousin, since her maiden name was also Fraser.

Captain Robert Paine (Durnford House 1935–40)

Killed in action in Burma on 8 July 1944, aged 23

Robert was born on 13 June 1921 to Jack Paine, a farmer, and his wife Helen (née Hadow), of Maidstone in Kent. An excellent shot, he became captain of the College Shooting VIII and Platoon Commander in the Officer Training Corps in 1939, the year war broke out. By the time he left the College he had also served as a School Prefect.

Robert was commissioned as an officer in 1941, joining the 3rd Battalion of the 1st Gurkha Regiment. In 1944 he travelled to Burma, where in March his battalion landed by glider behind enemy lines, with the task of disrupting Japanese lines of communication. Bitter fighting ensued, at times so close that men fought with bayonets, swords and knives, but the position was held. On 8 July the battalion attacked a Japanese defensive position and inflicted heavy casualties. However, during this action Major Paine was killed by a grenade. He is buried at the Rangoon War Cemetery.

Top: Flying Officer Gordon Fraser.

Above: Captain Robert Paine.

Flying Officer Eliot John Welchman RAFVR (Wilson's House 1931–34)

Killed in action in France on 13 July 1944, aged 27

Eliot was born on 2 October 1916 to Gerald Welchman, a former captain in the Indian Army, and his wife Mary (née Fernandez). He worked for a time in a local café at the railway station of Portslade-by-Sea, two miles west of Brighton. Welchman was 'a very cheerful chap' according to the son of the café's owner, but reticent about his personal life.

Welchman was killed in action in north-east France on 13 July 1944, while serving as a flying officer with 166 Squadron, flying Lancaster bombers from RAF Kirmington in Lincolnshire. He is buried in Prez-sur-Marne Churchyard.

Major Patrick Vernon Ward, MC and bars (Hampden House 1930–35)

Killed in action in France on 17 July 1944, aged 27

Patrick was born on 19 August 1916 in Marylebone, London, to Robert Ward, a soldier in the Royal Tank Corps who was killed in action in the Great War the year after Patrick's birth, and his wife Florence (née Villiers-Tuthill). At the College Patrick was in the 1st XV, 1st XI and Boxing VIII, and became Head of House. He then went on to Sandhurst, and was commissioned as a lieutenant in the 7th Royal Tank Regiment.

Ward first saw action in the Battle for France in 1940. He was eventually assigned to a small force with the mission of delaying the German advance to allow as many Allied forces as possible to escape to England. Ward was on one of the last boats out of Dunkirk, sharing a vessel, by chance, with Captain Walter Smith, who had been in command of his father's tank company when his father was killed in the previous war. Sir Basil Liddell-Hart, the military historian, later wrote:

> It may well be asked whether two battalions have ever had such a tremendous effect on history as 4RTR and 7RTR achieved by their action at Arras. Their effect in saving the British Army from being cut off from its escape port provides ample justification for the view that if two well-equipped armoured divisions had been available the Battle of France might also have been saved.

▶

Top: *Flying Officer Eliot John Welchman.*

Above: *Major Patrick Vernon Ward, MC and bars.*

Ward won the Military Cross for his conduct during these days. The citation referred to his 'bravery and resource on several occasions', mentioning in particular an engagement during which he knocked out two enemy armoured cars while under heavy fire before eventually managing to get the damaged tank back to Dunkirk.

In June 1941 he won a bar to his Military Cross while fighting in Libya. The citation read:

> His total disregard for his own safety prevented the enemy from breaking through and set a fine example to his troop.

During the Battle for Normandy in June 1944, Ward fought with the 153rd Royal Armoured Corps. He won a bar to his Military Cross (a second award for a separate act of heroism) for his actions on 16 July. The citation read:

> Throughout the day Major Ward was under heavy mortar and shellfire but showed complete disregard for personal safety and set a great example to his men.

Ward was killed the following day while showing similar selflessness. During an attack on a German position his gun jammed. On emerging from his tank to fix it he was shot and killed. He is buried at the Saint Manvieu War Cemetery in Normandy. According to *The Times* obituary:

> The French peasants still keep flowers on his grave. It is the sort of gesture he would have depreciated for himself.

Sub-Lieutenant Anthony Norman Clinch RNVR (Bristol House 1937–39)

Died in an air crash in the Mediterranean on 21 July 1944, aged 21

Born on 17 July 1923 in Edmonton, Middlesex, to William Clinch, an engineer, and his wife Alice (née Whittington), Anthony served with the Fleet Air Arm, the air branch of the Royal Navy, in the Second World War. The Fleet Air Arm played a key role in the defence of Malta, an important Allied base, during the 1940–42 Siege of Malta. Three of the most famous individual aircraft of the entire war, the Gloster Sea Gladiator fighters known as *Faith*, *Hope* and *Charity*, fought for the Fleet Air Arm in defence of Malta during this period. Fleet Air Arm units both attacked Axis shipping and supported the Allied invasion of Italy after the siege was lifted. It is not known when Clinch arrived in Malta, but in July 1944, while stationed at the Fleet Air Arm base at Saint Angelo, a fort in the centre of the Grand Harbour of Valletta, he went missing. He is commemorated at the Lee-on-Solent Fleet Air Arm Memorial in Hampshire.

Above: *Sub-Lieutenant Anthony Norman Clinch.*

Major Cecil James Alleyne Grove
(Stenning House 1921–25)

Died of wounds in Italy on 29 July 1944, aged 37

Cecil Grove (known as Jim to his family) was born on 21 July 1907 in Russia, to Henry Grove, a distinguished diplomat, later awarded the CBE, and his wife Lilian (née Hall). At the College he became Head of Stenning House.

On leaving the College, Cecil joined the army. In 1944 he was serving in the 2nd Battalion of the King's Regiment, part of the 4th Infantry Division commanded by fellow Old Brightonian Major-General Francis Tuker. In March the division landed on the German-occupied Italian mainland, which had been invaded by the Allies the previous year. Italy's mountainous terrain made the advance up the country slow, and the 2nd King's took part in the particularly tough fighting to capture Monte Cassino, part of the well-fortified Winter Line built by the Germans. Grove was wounded near Cortona, probably during the first week of July, as the battalion advanced on enemy lines. He died three weeks later of his wounds (not in September, as stated in the College Roll of Honour), and is buried at the Assisi War Cemetery.

Lieutenant Lenon Elton Hislop Tucker
(Bristol House 1937–40)

Killed in action in France on 3 August 1944, aged 21

Lenon was born on 22 January 1923 to Harry Tucker and his wife Marjorie (née Tucker), originally from the British West Indies. The bride and groom may have been cousins – other members of Marjorie's family were recorded over the years with the surname Tucker, which appears to have been a variant spelling. At the College he had a part in Gilbert and Sullivan's *Trial by Jury*.

During the war he served with the 5th Battalion of the Duke of Cornwall's Light Infantry. This unit took part in July 1944 in Operation *Jupiter*, a punishing battle to capture 'Hill 112' in Normandy, thereafter known more evocatively as Cornwall Hill in honour of the battalion, which suffered heavy casualties. Although the Allies did not manage to capture and hold the hill, the battle was regarded as an Allied victory because of the heavy losses inflicted on the II SS Panzer Corps during the engagement. Tucker survived this battle but within weeks was reported as missing, and later as killed. He is buried in the Saint Charles de Percy War Cemetery.

Top: *Major Cecil James Alleyne Grove's entry in the College Roll of Honour.*

Above: *Lieutenant Lenon Elton Hislop Tucker.*

Lieutenant-Colonel Paul Ewan Rodgers Dawson, MC (Junior School 1915–17 and School House 1920–25)

Died on active service in India on 4 August 1944, aged 36

Paul Dawson was born in Brighton on 15 February 1908, the son of Frances Dawson (née Sykes) and Canon William Dawson, Head Master of Brighton College at the time, and elder brother of Michael (see page 86). He joined the army after leaving the College, where he had been a School Prefect, and was commissioned as a lieutenant in the Royal Regiment of Artillery.

During the Second World War he won the Military Cross and reached the rank of lieutenant-colonel with the 21st Mountain Regiment of the Royal Indian Artillery. He fought in India and Burma and died on active service in August 1944. Dawson was mentioned in despatches after his death, and is buried in the Ranchi War Cemetery in India.

Lieutenant-Colonel Walter Brian Stewart (originally Heweston), DSO, MC (Gordon House 1922–25)

Died on active service in France on 5 August 1944, aged 36

Walter was born in Durban, South Africa, on 21 July 1908 to Walter Philip Heweston, a sea captain, and his wife Violette (née Cornioly), but moved to London at the age of three. When he was ten years old his father died, and his mother married Harold Stewart, originally from Rhodesia, one year later. After three years at the College, where he did well academically, he won a scholarship to the Royal Military Academy, Woolwich, and then joined the Norfolk Yeomanry Anti-Tank Regiment of the Royal Artillery.

In August 1941 he earned the Military Cross, for 'conspicuous success' in commanding his anti-tank unit between April and July. The citation read:

> In all these actions the troops of 'D' Bty [Battery] have fought with conspicuous gallantry and determination and have inflicted severe casualties on enemy tanks and armoured cars, and rendered invaluable support to our own troops.

Only four months later he also earned the Distinguished Service Order, for his conduct during the Battle of Sidi Rezegh in Libya in November of that year. The citation read:

> Although under very heavy fire Major Stewart continued to coordinate and direct his A/TK [anti-tank] guns and by his complete disregard for his own safety and his gallant and cheerful bearing inspired his gunners with confidence.

Above: *Lieutenant-Colonel Paul Ewan Rodgers Dawson, MC.*

He died on active service on 5 August 1944, two months after the Allies had landed in northern France, and is buried at the Banneville-la-Campagne War Cemetery in Normandy, leaving a widow, Sybil, who was originally from Nairobi in Kenya.

Flying Officer John Bigland Tulk-Hart Bigland (School House 1923–27)

Killed on active service in France on 8 August 1944, aged 34

John Bigland was born on 20 August 1909 to Thomas Tulk-Hart of Blackbarrow, Lancashire, and his wife Madeline (née Bigland). During the war he served as a flying officer in the RAF, in 69 Squadron.

During the 1944 Normandy campaign the squadron conducted night reconnaissance, using flares to locate enemy troop movements – because of the Allies' air superiority it was safer for the Germans to move at night. Bigland was killed on active service during this period (not in 1945, as in the College Roll of Honour), leaving a wife, Miza, and is buried in Breel Churchyard in Normandy.

Top: *1923 Gordon House photograph. Walter Stewart's position is unknown, but Michael James is sitting cross-legged in front, 2nd from right (see page 161).*

Above: *Flying Officer John Bigland's entry in the College Roll of Honour.*

Lieutenant Gavin Heriot Galbraith (Hampden House 1937–42)

Killed in action in France on 11 August 1944, aged 21

Gavin was born on 13 July 1923 in Kingston, Surrey, to Alan Galbraith, an accountant, and his wife Irene (née Heriot). On leaving the College, where he was Head of House, a member of the 1st XV, captain of the Shooting VIII and an enthusiastic stamp collector and reader, he went to Queens' College, Cambridge, for six months on a special course in engineering for cadets in the Royal Engineers.

In June 1944 Galbraith was sent to France, where he was killed in the ultimately successful attempt to break out of Normandy, on the very same day that he had written his last letter to his parents. He is buried in La Délivrande War Cemetery. A letter from his father to Walter Hett slips poignantly, out of force of habit or perhaps a lingering unwillingness to accept reality, into the present tense:

> He is so proud of his School and thinks so much of his Head and his other Masters.

Captain Günther Guhl (Hampden House 1934–38)

Killed in action in France on 27 August 1944, aged 24

Günther is the only known fallen Old Brightonian who fought for the Axis side. Born on 24 May 1921, he lived in Hove and attended the College while his father worked as the UK head of IG Farben, the German chemical firm. He then went on to the University of Geneva.

He was conscripted during the war, and by 1943 was serving with the 10th Panzer Grenadier Regiment. He died when his tank was hit, probably by an American fighter plane, near Reims, where, some eight months later, the German Army surrendered to the Allies. Guhl is buried in a French cemetery.

His status as a fallen Old Brightonian was discovered by the Head of History, Martin Jones, in 1997. Pondering whether to include Guhl on the official roll of honour of war dead in the College Chapel, the school contacted 32 Old Boys who had served in the war, every one of whom was in favour. Four Old Boys even asked for the address of Günther's brother Wolfgang in order to meet him. Wolfgang wrote to the Head Master at the time, John Leach, and thanked the school, saying:

> The spirit in which you do this really does touch my heart. I suppose it is quite natural for you English – as I know you – not to show any rancour to others, whoever they might be.

Top: *Lieutenant Gavin Heriot Galbraith.*

Above: *Captain Günther Guhl.*

Captain James Charles Hollebone
(Wilson's House 1927–31)

Killed in action in Italy on 5 September 1944, aged 31

James was born on 19 July 1913 in Hampstead, Middlesex, to Ralph Hollebone and his wife Adela (née MacAlister). James joined the military three years after leaving the College, in 1934. A month into the Second World War, in October 1939, he married Phoebe Howitt. They had a son, Neil, in 1942.

During the war James served in the 1st Battalion of the Gordon Highlanders and was killed fighting the Germans in Italy. Based on his date of death and place of burial, he must have been killed during the ultimate successful attempt to break through German forces' Gothic Line. He is buried in the Gradara War Cemetery. Two years after James died, his wife married his brother, Derek, and they had two more children.

Lieutenant-Colonel John Anthony Colson Fitch
(Walpole House 1926–30)

Killed in action in the Netherlands on 19 September 1944, aged 32

John Fitch was born on 14 August 1912 in Sheringham, Norfolk, to Charles Fitch, a bank cashier, and his wife Florence (née Sadd). Joining the army in 1933, he took part in the ill-fated 1940 Battle of France, and then in the victorious Allied advance in north-west Europe in 1944. However, the Allies suffered a temporary check at Arnhem in the Netherlands in September 1944, where Fitch commanded the 3rd Battalion of the 1st Parachute Brigade. Trapped near Arnhem Bridge, Fitch ordered his men to run back in twos and threes to the town's Rhine Pavilion about 250 yards away. Many of the men arrived safely, but Fitch was killed by a mortar bomb. He is buried in the Arnhem Oosterbeek War Cemetery.

Top: *Captain James Charles Hollebone.*

Above: *Lieutenant-Colonel John Anthony Colson Fitch.*

Sergeant Roger Brockwell Ward
(Chichester House 1939–41)

Missing, presumed dead, on a bombing mission over Germany on 23 September 1944, aged 20

Roger was born on 22 August 1924 to George Ward, a clerk at the Bank of England, and his wife Constance (née Brockwell), of Streatham in London. At the College he was in the water polo and swimming teams.

Roger joined the RAF straight after school, and was assigned to 166 Squadron, based at Kirmington in Lincolnshire, flying Lancaster bombers over Germany. On 23 September 1944 the squadron was sent on one such mission, but his plane never returned. There are competing theories as to where the plane was lost; one is that it is the aircraft that came down that night over the Dutch town of Zelhem, en route to Germany.

Ward is commemorated at the Runnymede Air Forces Memorial to air force personnel with no known grave. Intriguingly, however, it is just possible that he does have a burial place: the Dutch created a grave in Zelhem Cemetery to an unknown airman, where rest the remains of one or more of the crew in the plane that was downed on that date.

Lieutenant John Desmond Fleetwood
(Hampden House 1936–39)

Died on active service in Italy on 7 October 1944, aged 21

John was born on 22 July 1923 to James Fleetwood and his wife Gertrude (née Halliday). He enlisted in the Royal Sussex Regiment during the war, but was later attached to the 15th Battalion of the Hampshire Regiment, which took part in the invasion of mainland Italy at Salerno in 1943, and then in the slow and bitter struggle up to the north of the country. In August 1944 the battalion participated in the assault on the German forces' Gothic Line, in heavy rain and mud. The line was breached, and the battalion made it across the River Rubicon, just as Caesar famously had almost two millennia before, though in the other direction. However, Fleetwood died in the last days of this particular campaign, and is buried at the Assisi Military Cemetery.

Top: *Sergeant Roger Brockwell Ward.*

Above: *Lieutenant John Desmond Fleetwood.*

Brigadier Henry John Anthony Thicknesse, DSO (School House 1914–17)

Died of wounds in the Netherlands on 23 October 1944, aged 44

John Anthony, known to all as Tony, was born on the last day of the 19th century to John Audley Thicknesse, a lieutenant-colonel in the army who was killed on the first day of the Battle of the Somme, and his wife Phyllis (née Woodcock), of Cuckfield, Sussex. He won a Divinity prize at the College, and was also a member of the Debating Society at the same time as Aubertin Mallaby (see page 165).

He initially wanted to become a doctor, but the death of his father changed his plans by leaving his family without the means to pay for his training, so he joined the army, serving with the Royal Artillery. In 1928 he married Joyce Tupman, who bore him four children: Margaret, Joyce, Jane and Philip.

During the war he took part in the Western Desert campaign, during which he received the Distinguished Service Order. The citation read that he carried out 'a series of daring and skilful reconnaissances of the enemy's position' over 'bare stony desert' in an area 'infested by low-flying ME 109s which, on one occasion, shot the front tyres of his Jeep to pieces'. Dangerous adventure in a jeep was, it appears, a Thicknesse habit: he also drove a jeep through enemy fire to see his brother Ralph for the last time in the Western Desert and, in 1944, while in command of the 59th Army Group Royal Artillery in the Netherlands, took one on a reconnaissance of the enemy position. On that occasion, the habit proved his undoing: he was wounded and captured by the Germans, and died of complications from his wound.

Above: The 51st Highland Division Plans El Alamein, *by Ian G. M. Eadie, 1949. Thicknesse is included in the picture.*

The post-war postscript to his death shows the vast wellspring of humanity that survived the war in Europe, despite the suffering and cruelty. His family was contacted by the nurse who had looked after him, Ank Stumpel, who stayed with them for three months, telling them of how happy Thicknesse had been with his family life, and by the German doctor who had treated him, who explained the circumstances of his death. Thicknesse is buried at Dordrecht General Cemetery in Holland. He is a distant cousin of Oliver Thicknesse, a Classics master at the College at the time of writing.

Captain Prince Dimitri Galitzine (Durnford House 1931–35)

Died of wounds in the Netherlands on 26 October 1944, aged 26

There have been few Old Brightonians with a background as exotic and grand as that of Prince Dimitri Galitzine, born on 16 November 1917 in Kislovodsk, Russia, to Countess Marie, daughter of Duke Georg Alexander of Mecklenburg-Strelitz, and Prince Boris Dmitrievich Galitzine, a captain in the Imperial Russian Army's Hussar Guards.

By the age of two Prince Dimitri had lost his father in a fatal battle against the Bolsheviks, and his mother was forced to flee her homeland aboard a Royal Navy ship together with Dimitri and his baby sister. They settled eventually in England.

Galitzine enlisted in the British Army in 1939 and was commissioned as an officer, undertaking several training courses in guerrilla and irregular warfare. In July 1944 he was posted to the Monmouthshire Battalion in north-west Europe. In October 1944 the battalion took part in the successful liberation of the town of 's-Hertogenbosch in the Netherlands, but it cost Galitzine his life – he was fatally wounded, and died the following day. He is buried at Uden War Cemetery.

Lieutenant John Henry Lloyd Sulman, DSC, MBE RNVR (Durnford House 1924–25)

Killed in action off Belgium on 2 November 1944, aged 35

John Sulman, known as Jacko, was born on 22 July 1909 to James Sulman and his wife Lilian (née Minnis), from south-west London. After a year at Brighton College, Jacko worked in commerce in London and then Birmingham.

Keen to do his bit when war broke out, he volunteered for the Royal Navy and drove an ambulance while waiting to be called up. He also visited factories, giving workers pep talks to boost morale. During one of these visits he met his future wife, Zillah, known as Bunnie.

Above: *Captain Prince Dimitri Galitzine.*

In October 1943 Jacko received the Distinguished Service Cross for his duties on minesweepers. On 2 November 1944 he was in charge of the minesweeper *Colsay* when she was torpedoed off Belgium, killing all but one of the crew. After his death Jacko was awarded an MBE for his bravery and command during a friendly fire incident when he helped pull men from the water. He is commemorated at the Lowestoft Naval Memorial in Suffolk.

Jacko left behind not only his widow and daughter Julia, but also his son John, born two months after his death. After the war Bunnie married Jacko's younger brother, Hugh (known as Bill), and had three more children: Sarah, Jane and Robert.

Flight Lieutenant Charles Patrick O'Connor RAFVR (Hampden B House 1933–37)

Missing, presumed dead, on a training flight departing from Northern Ireland on 13 November 1944, aged 25

Charles O'Connor was born on 13 August 1919 in Marylebone, London, to Charles O'Connor and his wife Constance (née Price). During the war he served with RAF Coastal Command. By November 1944 O'Connor was listed as a crew member on a Wellington LORAN Training Unit, training personnel in the long-range radio navigation system developed by the United States. On 13 November his plane took off at just after midnight from RAF Mullaghmore, near Ballymoney, County Antrim, on a training exercise. Nothing further was heard from the aircraft. O'Connor left a widow, Mary, and is commemorated at the Runnymede Air Forces Memorial.

Top: *John Henry Lloyd Sulman (right), with his brother Hugh (left).*

Above: *1937 Hampden House photograph.*

Wing Commander Alexander Cunninghame Pearson, DFC (UK and US) (Gordon House 1922–24)

Killed in a plane crash in England on 29 November 1944, aged 37

Alexander was born on 16 September 1907 in Buenos Aires to John, a member of an Australian cattle ranching family who had come to Argentina to ply the same trade on the country's pampas, and his wife Emily (née Sewell), an Argentinian of British stock. Pearson was an active sportsman at the College, with a place in the school's top swimming team, the 1st VI.

Pearson qualified as a pilot officer in the RAF in 1928, and remained in the force until 1932, when he moved to Kenya to work as a commercial airline pilot. His adventures included the rescue of an American hunter, one Ernest Hemingway, who was suffering from dysentery and needing urgent medical care. Hemingway immortalised both incident and pilot in his short story 'The Snows of Kilimanjaro'. The pilot, known in the story as Compton, is an English gentleman with a jolly air, wearing a tweed jacket and felt hat.

During the war Pearson served in the RAF. In 1943, as head of 194 Squadron, he dropped supplies in Burma to the Chindits, an Allied force behind Japanese lines. In a sign of Pearson's leadership style, 194 Squadron earned the nickname 'the Friendly Firm'. In 1944 he earned both the British and American Distinguished Flying Crosses for his role in an airborne invasion of British troops, again behind enemy lines, to help US forces in northern Burma.

By November 1944 he was a flying instructor in rural England. One morning he flew to Biggin Hill air base, near London, to have lunch with his brother, Air Commodore Herbert Pearson, and old friends from the Far East. On taking off afterwards, he failed to remove the elevator lock. This made it impossible for him to control the plane, and he crashed. He is buried at the parish church of St Peter and St Paul in nearby Cudham.

What acquaintances remember most about Pearson was the force of his personality. After a 1984 London reunion of 194 Squadron members and Chindits, a member wrote in the squadron alumni newsletter: 'Amidst all the talk, laughter and speeches, the invisible presence of the indomitable Fatty Pearson was almost tangible.'

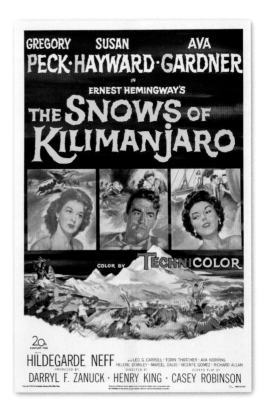

Top: *Wing Commander Alexander Cunninghame Pearson, DFC.*

Above: *Poster for the 1952 film,* The Snows of Kilimanjaro.

Major Samuel Marsland Ginn (Walpole House 1927–31)

Died on active service in the Netherlands on 3 December 1944, aged 32

Samuel was born on 21 October 1912 to Dennis Ginn, scion of a wealthy family of lawyers and landowners, and his wife Dorothy (née Brooke), of Cambridge. After leaving the College he read law at Trinity Hall, Cambridge, and was admitted into the family firm.

During the Second World War he served with the 190th Field Regiment of the Royal Artillery, rising to acting lieutenant-colonel, and died on active service in or around Venray in the Netherlands, the site of many battles against the Germans in the closing stages of the war, on 3 December 1944. Samuel left a widow, Phyllis. He is buried at the Venray War Cemetery.

Lieutenant John Wilfred Aldrich (School House 1935–41)

Killed in action in Italy on 23 December 1944, aged 22

John Aldrich was born on 30 January 1922 in Steyning, near Brighton, to Horace Wilfred Aldrich, a solicitor, and his wife Hermine Aldrich (née Miller). He won a scholarship to the College, and eventually became Head of School.

During the war he served with the Royal Sussex Regiment. By November 1944 Aldrich was fighting in Tuscany. He was killed in action on 23 December on the outskirts of a village called Picciame, and is buried in the Santerno Valley War Graves Cemetery. He was survived by his father, the long-time chairman of the College Council, who had himself narrowly escaped death in the previous war after being blown up and buried alive.

JOHN WILFRED ALDRICH

Those who were at the School in the years just before the outbreak of war will be grieved to hear of the death in action of John Aldrich, the younger son of the Chairman of Brighton College Council, and Mrs. Aldrich, of Lloyd Road, Hove. He entered the School from Prestonville in 1935 and quickly made his mark among his contemporaries. His outstanding personality brought him to the post of Head of the School, and in that capacity he took a prominent part in all aspects of School life. In particular, he took special interest in the Shakespearean and Play-Reading Societies, and was a leading figure in the Musical Society. He was Under Officer in the Junior Training Corps, and when the Home Guard Section was formed, he was among its keenest members.

On leaving School in 1941 he entered into residence at Wadham College, Oxford, where he read Law and, after joining the Army, was given six months' leave of absence to continue his work. He was commissioned in the Royal Sussex Regiment, and went to North Africa, though with another regiment, and then to Italy, where he was killed.

His powers of leadership were considerable and made him a first-rate regimental officer, and would have ensured for him a brilliant career had he been spared. We extend our most sincere sympathy to Mr. and Mrs. Aldrich in the loss of a son of whom they can be justly proud.

Top: *Major Samuel Marsland Ginn.*

Above: *Lieutenant John Wilfred Aldrich.*

Above, right: *John Aldrich's obituary in the March 1945* Brightonian *magazine.*

1945

Flight Lieutenant Peter Wyatt-Smith
(Durnford House 1932–35)

Killed in a plane crash in England on 5 January 1945, aged 26

Born in China on 9 June 1918 to Stanley, a diplomat serving in the country, and Mabel, in 1932 Peter returned to England to live in Hastings and attend the College. After leaving he joined a law firm as an articled clerk in Lewes, before enlisting with the RAF in 1938 and joining 263 Squadron, flying fighter planes. He served in Norway until the Allied withdrawal, during which he was wounded in the leg while aboard the SS *Delius*, which endured six gruelling hours of bombing and strafing by German planes.

Wyatt-Smith later fought in the Battle of Britain and the Mediterranean, and by 1945 was based back in England, flying the Mustang fighter bomber for 165 Squadron. On 5 January his plane stalled on take-off at RAF Aston Down in Gloucestershire, and he died in the ensuing crash. Peter left a widow, Helen, and is buried at Haycombe Cemetery in Somerset.

Captain Kenneth David Gordon Phillips
(Bristol House 1936–40)

Killed in action in Burma on 6 January 1945, aged 22

Born on 16 June 1922 in India to Violet Phillips (née Gordon, great-niece of General Charles Gordon, the iconic Victorian hero killed at Khartoum) and Major Herbert Phillips, Kenneth, known to all as David, joined the College in 1936, becoming House Prefect and a member of the 1st XV. He played soldiers continually as a little boy. Not content to wait for his 18th birthday, when he could become a soldier in the main army, he did a spell in the Home Guard while awaiting his call-up papers with the Royal Engineers. He then volunteered to go to Burma.

Phillips was killed in an ambush while on reconnaissance near Budalin in January 1945, in the first of five days of bitter fighting to capture the town from the Japanese. His younger sister Josephine later recalled the moment when David's death was confirmed:

> I was in my darkened bedroom early one morning when I heard my mother coming up the stairs, sobbing, 'Oh God, it's all over.' I took the telegram from her hand. The War Office regretted that her son, Captain K.D.G. Phillips, R.E., had been killed in action at Budalin, Burma, on the 6th of January 1945. She clung to

Top: Flight Lieutenant Peter Wyatt-Smith.

Above: Captain Kenneth David Gordon Phillips.

me, saying 'I always knew I was going to lose him. I'm so glad I've got you, you are so like him.' Like him, perhaps, but never in a million years would I have his courage.

His commanding officer, Major Prichard, wrote to his parents:

> Our memory of David will always be of a keen officer, bounding with energy, who, not being content with life in a depot, asked to be sent to a theatre of operations.

His family received many letters from College staff. Josephine's favourite was from David's housemaster's daughter, Anne Corbett, who recalled:

> Everywhere that David was, all was gaiety and laughter, and that is how I shall remember him.

He is buried in the Taukkyan War Cemetery in Myanmar (Burma).

Flight Lieutenant Frank Dare Holdsworth (Durnford House 1931–35)

Killed in a plane crash in England on 10 February 1945, aged 27

Frank was born on 25 February 1917 in Kings Norton, Worcestershire, to Gilbert Holdsworth and his wife Adelaide (née Chambers). At the College he was a keen footballer, playing for the 1st XI for his final two years, and also became a School Prefect.

On 10 February 1945 he was flying his RAF Mosquito fighter back from action when he crashed in Lincolnshire. His plane was thought to be short of fuel, possibly due to damage from anti-aircraft fire or aerial combat during the mission. His younger brother and only sibling, John (see page 88), had already perished over the North Sea three years before while also flying for the RAF. Holdsworth is buried in Chislehurst Cemetery in Bromley, London.

Top: *Taukkyan War Cemetery, Myanmar.*

Above, left: *Frank Dare Holdsworth, in the 1933 Chichester House photograph.*

Above, right: *Mosquito aircraft over England.*

Lance Corporal John Arnold Remilley Barder
(Hampden House 1936–38)

Killed in action in the Netherlands on 14 February 1945, aged 23

John was born in Leicester on 24 August 1922 to Louis Barder and his wife Madge (née Alverez). The family moved to Hove, and Barder attended the College for two years from 1936. During the war he was with the Royal Engineers. As a member of 79 Assault Squadron, he would have served very much on the front line. In February 1945 he was killed in action in the Netherlands, where fighting remained heavy in pockets right up until the end of the war in Europe. Barder is buried in the Jonkerbos British War Cemetery.

Flying Officer Raymond Julius Guy Manning
(Leconfield House 1938–41)

Killed in a plane crash in Italy on 19 February 1945, aged 21

Raymond (known as Ray) was born in Winchester on 8 September 1923, to Julius Manning and his wife Oriel (née Currie). During the war he flew the Westland Lysander army cooperation and liaison aircraft for 148 Special Duties (Special Operations Executive) Squadron in Italy, tasked with dropping off and collecting agents from territories occupied by the enemy. Ray was probably chosen for this role because he could speak German, Hungarian and Serbo-Croat, having spent his early years in Yugoslavia. He flew missions into Yugoslavia and France.

Ray met Diana Portman, known as Dipsy, while both were serving in Italy – Diana was also in the Special Operations Executive. They married in Florence on 4 February 1945. Fifteen days later the couple were returning from their honeymoon in a Lockheed Hudson bound for Capodichino, near Naples. The aircraft's port engine failed completely, and the plane crashed, killing all on board. Ray and Dipsy are buried at the Florence War Cemetery. Their epitaph, chosen by Dipsy's SOE comrade Sue Ryder, later a famous charity worker, reads:

They were lovely & pleasant in their lives and in their death they were not divided.

Top: *Lance Corporal John Arnold Remilley Barder.*
Above: *Flying Officer Raymond Julius Guy Manning.*

Captain Clifford Lesley Curtis-Willson
(School House 1932–36)

Died of wounds on 12 March 1945 after his aircraft was shot down over Germany, aged 26

Born on 21 July 1918 in Hackney, London, to William Curtis-Willson (made Sir William in 1933, after he organised an important festival in Brighton) and his wife Irene (née Robey), Clifford was a Prefect and editor of the school magazine at the College. He was also in the 2nd XV and Swimming VIII, as well as being Platoon Commander in the OTC.

During the war he served with the RAF's 660 Squadron, and was deployed to France after the 1944 invasion of Normandy as a Royal Artillery Air Observation Post Pilot. On 11 March 1945 he was flying his unarmed Auster observation aircraft when he was shot down by a German fighter plane. Curtis-Willson crashed, and died of his wounds the following morning. He is buried at the Groesbeek Canadian War Cemetery in the Netherlands.

Lieutenant Michael Fitzgibbon James RNVR
(Gordon House 1923–24)

Died following an accident while on active service in Australia on 22 March 1945, aged 35

Michael was born on 25 July 1909 in Highgate, Middlesex, to Russell James, a businessman, and his wife Isabel (née Hindson). At the College he appeared in Gilbert and Sullivan's *The Sorcerer* (as one of the 'women and girls of the village' according to the school magazine, alongside Harold Hobday – see page 48).

During the war he served as a lieutenant in the Royal Naval Volunteer Reserve. The last ship on which he served was HMS *Formidable*, an aircraft carrier assigned to the British Pacific Fleet in 1945, and stationed in Sydney. On 22 March 1945, James was on shore leave with some shipmates when they were involved in a road accident, shortly before the ship sailed north to attack airfields on outlying Japanese islands in preparation for a final assault on mainland Japan. He was taken to hospital but later died from his injuries and is buried in the Sydney War Cemetery.

Top: *Captain Clifford Lesley Curtis-Willson.*

Above: *Michael Fitzgibbon James, in the 1923 Gordon House photograph.*

Flying Officer Robert Alfred Scrase (School House 1938–41)

Killed in action in Germany on 24 March 1945, aged 20

Robert was born on 17 June 1924 to Harry Scrase, a poultry farmer who had served in the Great War, and his wife Ethel (née Sinfield). By the outbreak of the Second World War his father is recorded as living apart from his wife and son, at a nursing home run by his two unmarried sisters in Burgess Hill. Robert spent three years at the College, becoming a School Prefect.

During the war Scrase joined the Glider Pilot Regiment. After training in Canada, he took part in his first combat mission on 24 March 1945: Operation *Varsity*, the successful attempt to land 16,000 paratroopers to assist with the crossing of the Rhine and Allied entry into the heart of Germany. Although mortally wounded, he landed his load of troops safely, probably saving the lives of many men. Scrase is buried at the Reichswald Forest War Cemetery in Germany.

FLYING OFFICER ROBERT ALFRED SCRASE

His Commanding Officer writes :—

" While making our approach for landing (East of the Rhine) we were subjected to rather heavy enemy fire, and it was during the approach that F-O. Scrase was wounded by enemy fire directed at the gliders. In spite of his wounds he managed to land his aircraft and its load safely, but he died shortly after landing. There was nothing his friends could do to save him, and I feel it is tragic that he should have lost his life after successfully completing his task as Pilot of the Glider."

Top: *Robert Scrase's commanding officer relates his death in the July 1945 issue of the* Brightonian *magazine.*

Above: *1940 School House photograph.*

Squadron Leader Edward Geoffrey Pannell (Hampden B House 1933–35)

Died on active service in Burma on 22 April 1945, aged 25

Edward was born in Hove on 15 December 1919, the son of Ebenezer Pannell, who ran a photography business, and his wife Kathleen (née Nutley). By April 1945 he was in command of 28 Squadron, an RAF fighter unit taking part in the Burma campaign. He died on 22 April, while the Allies, having increasingly gained the upper hand against the Japanese over the past year, were advancing on the capital, Rangoon. He was mentioned in despatches after his death, and is commemorated at the Singapore Memorial.

Lieutenant Douglas Raymond Prins (subsequently changed to Prince) (Wilson's House 1931–34)

Died in England on 16 July 1945, aged 27

Douglas was born in Watergraafsmeer, part of the city of Amsterdam, the Netherlands, on 14 September 1917 to Peter Prins, an employee of the Firestone Tire and Rubber Export Co. His guardian when he entered the College was not his mother or father but a C. P. Vickers of Seaford in Sussex. By February 1935, his father was the owner of a hotel in Devon.

By the time Douglas joined the British Army's Durham Light Infantry in 1939 he had anglicised his surname to Prince, perhaps out of a fear that he might be considered to be of German ancestry, though his original surname is actually Dutch.

Douglas was described by his battalion commander as 'a young officer of the highest calibre' and a 'constant source of inspiration'; but he had a frustrating war. Captured while defending the rear at Dunkirk, he spent the next five years as a prisoner. In February 1941 the College magazine jubilantly reported that he had been captured rather than killed, and noted 'that friends would do him a very great kindness if they would write to him'. He was probably not mistreated – most British, and indeed American, prisoners were treated humanely by the Germans – but he nevertheless died in July 1945, soon after repatriation, at the early age of 27. It is possible that he never recovered from wounds incurred in the French campaign, just like Sir Edmund Nuttall (see page 68). However, in the short time left to him after his return to England he married Jacqueline Fisher in Oxford. We can surmise that she had been waiting for him those five long years, and that, with both Jacqueline and Douglas aware that he was dying, they decided to marry quickly in order to snatch a few weeks of married bliss. Prince is buried in the Oxford (Headington) Cemetery.

Top: *Singapore Memorial.*

Above: *Douglas Raymond Prince, in the 1932 Wilson's House cross country team photograph.*

Lieutenant Edward Cyril Lawrence Young (Durnford House 1925–28)

Died on active service in England on 24 July 1945, aged 33

Edward was born in south-east London on 1 August 1911 to Edward Young and his wife Edith (née Humphry). In 1933 he married Margaret Densham in Deptford, London. At the College, Young was a member of the Shooting VIII in 1927 and 1928. This was an era when the College was the best school for marksmanship in the country, heading the averages in the national shooting competition for schools at Bisley every year between 1926 and 1936. In Young's first year in the team, the College brought home all eight Bisley trophies.

During the war Young served with the Royal Corps of Signals. At the time of his death he was in 8 Air Formation Signals. Lieutenant Young died in England after the war in Europe had finished, but while still serving with the unit, on 24 July 1945, and is buried in the churchyard of St John's, Coulsdon.

Major Warwick Thompson (Brighton College Preparatory School and School House 1927–37)

Died from wounds received in the Burma campaign on 30 July 1945, aged 25

Warwick was born in Brighton on 6 July 1920, to Percy Thompson, a bookie, and his wife Hetty (née Baynard). At the College he punched for the Boxing VIII. In July 1940 he enlisted in the Royal Horse Guards, and the following year was commissioned as an officer. A note from a brigadier on his discharge papers from officer training, marked 'Suitable for India', shows the widespread snobbery of the time (note the reference to his public school, which the brigadier appears to deem sufficiently grand) but also the desire for officers with the common touch:

My dear Forester, A very nice boy I know wants to enlist into your regiment – was at Brighton College – has a lot of friends in the ranks. His name is Warwick Thompson – the son of a bookmaker – but different class to the ordinary run – His father also is different class. Allen Stanley knows him and vetted him and is satisfied about him – Could you be a good fellow & put the machinery in motion.

He was assigned to the 4th Battalion, 15th Punjab Regiment. By April 1945 he was an acting major, and died from wounds received in Burma on 30 July 1945. He is buried in the Taukkyan War Cemetery in Myanmar (Burma).

Top: *Lieutenant Edward Cyril Lawrence Young, in the 1927 Brighton College OTC shooting team photograph.*

Above: *Major Warwick Thompson.*

Brigadier Aubertin Walter Sothern Mallaby, OBE, CIE (Companion of the Most Eminent Order of the Indian Empire) (Junior School and School House, 1912–17)

Killed during civil unrest in the Dutch East Indies on 30 October 1945, aged 45

Aubertin was born on 12 December 1899, the son of William Mallaby, actor, unsuccessful gambler and confidence trickster. Nurtured by a devoted mother, Katharine (née Miller), Mallaby won a scholarship to Brighton College, where he was a School Prefect and Head of House. His sense of mischief must have made him popular among his schoolfellows. Aubertin's brother, who became Sir George Mallaby, headmaster and public servant, recalled in his memoirs:

> He was the king of nonsense and to this day I can laugh outright and uncontrolled at much of our boyhood silliness.

In 1917 Mallaby joined the Indian Army. By 1943 he was Acting Major General and Director of Military Operations at General Headquarters India. By this time he had married Margaret Jones, known as Mollie, and had three children: Christopher, later Sir Christopher, who served as ambassador to France and Germany, Antony and Susan. Sir Christopher recalled: 'The last words he ever said to me were: "Look after Mummy". I hope that this unforgettable remark influenced my own behaviour to my own mother.' Mollie gave her new husband the more commonplace name Peter against his wishes, and the name stuck.

It was only after the formal end of the war that the most dramatic, and strangest, chapter of his life began. On 25 October 1945 his ship arrived at Tanjung Perak, the port of Surabaya in Java, carrying approximately 4,500 lightly armed men from the 49th Indian Brigade. Mallaby's main task was to rescue 16,000 Dutch prisoners of war, as well as numerous women and children, from the city. The Dutch East Indies had been retaken from the Japanese, but the local people wanted independence, and had taken control of Surabaya.

Initially, matters went well, but on 27 October disaster struck. Thousands of leaflets produced by British Divisional HQ were dropped by planes over Surabaya, effectively declaring martial law. Mallaby was apparently left speechless for several minutes after reading them. His new orders were to take the city by force and impose martial law. The leaflets caused uproar and savage fighting broke out between the Nationalists and the 49th Indian Brigade. A temporary ceasefire was agreed, and Mallaby headed back into the city to try to implement it, end the fighting, and keep his troops safe.

Mallaby's last words as he left HQ for this mission were: 'If any of us get killed, splash it all over the world.' He headed back into the main town square in his car. Most urgently, 6th Battalion of the 5th Manrattas had been caught up in a fight defending the International Bank Building, and needed assistance. As Sir Christopher, his son, later recounted:

▶

■ Above: *Brigadier Aubertin Walter Sothern Mallaby, OBE, CIE.*

Father had got out of the car and crossed the square on foot, mobbed by people. The three officers with him were disarmed. Then it got very nasty... Some very young activists came to the car. Dad asked for the senior activists... but a 17-year-old killed [shot] my father.

The death of Mallaby caused an uproar. Highly laudatory obituaries came flooding in. Major-General Francis Tuker, a fellow Old Brightonian and future governor of the College who knew Mallaby from serving in South Asia, wrote in the school magazine's obituary:

In the British army it is often stated that no-one is indispensable or irreplaceable. It can confidently be stated that at this time Mallaby is an exception to this rule.

The British responded by despatching an entire division to capture the city, in the three-week Battle of Surabaya, though shortly afterwards they withdrew from Indonesia for good. Mallaby is buried at the Commonwealth Military Cemetery in Jakarta.

John Robert Lyon Fellowes (Hampden House 1925–30)

Died of a disease contracted during the Western Desert campaign on 8 December 1945, aged 34

John was born on 10 November 1911 in Satara, India, to James Fellowes, a colonel in the Indian Army, and his wife Nora (née Moore). By 1920 the family was back in England, living in Steyning, near Brighton, and in 1925 John started at the College, where he eventually became a School Prefect. In July 1930 he went to Pembroke College, Cambridge, to read mathematics.

After leaving Cambridge, Fellowes took the unusual step for an Old Brightonian of becoming a pirate: specifically, a radio pirate with Radio Normandie, transmitting jazz into the United Kingdom from the safety of a ship off the coast of France.

In 1940 Fellowes joined the Rifle Brigade. He was severely wounded during the Western Desert Campaign at the First Battle of El Alamein in July 1942, when his jeep was blown up by a mine, destroying one leg and mangling the other. Worse still, sand entered his lungs during the incident, worsening his pre-existing silicosis, a disease that can be brought on by inhaling desert sand. Fellowes was invalided home, where he made a partial recovery and returned to duties away from the front line. In 1943 he became the liaison officer to *The Way Ahead*, a wartime propaganda film starring David Niven. However, his health worsened again and he died of silicosis in 1945 at his family's cottage in Steyning.

Above: John Robert Lyon Fellowes, in the 1933 Prefects photograph. ∎

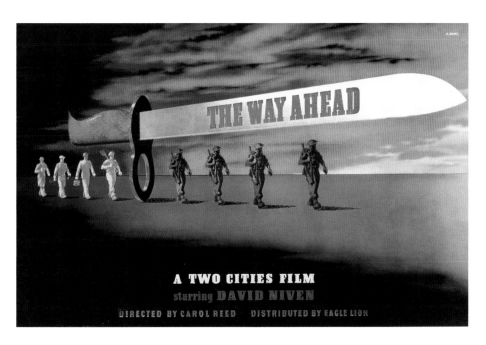

Major Harry Marshall Ford, MC
(Stenning House 1925–28)

Committed suicide in England, traumatised by experience as a Japanese prisoner of war, on 7 July 1946, aged 35

The last death recorded in this book is also perhaps the saddest.

Harry was born on 19 May 1911 in Yorkshire to Harry Ford, a horse dealer, and his wife Ellen. In 1937 Harry, by this time a sales manager, married Doris Whiting, a former beauty queen of Louth in Lincolnshire who was described in the local paper, in true fairy tale style, as 'one of the most lovely young women in the county and famed for her beauty far afield'.

Ford was a man of great bravery, earning the Military Cross at Dunkirk in 1940. The following year he was captured by the Japanese during the Malaya campaign while serving with the 88th Regiment of the Royal Artillery, and held prisoner in terrible conditions while building the Burma Railway.

Ford had long been a mercurial character. However, his experience of life as a prisoner of the Japanese appears to have aggravated his condition. He separated from Doris and on 6 July 1946 he met with his wife to discuss divorce, but the discussion ended in a row. The following day he shot himself in a hotel in York. The coroner delivered a verdict that he killed himself while the balance of his mind was disturbed, probably because of his experiences as a prisoner of war. Ford's remains are at the Nottingham Crematorium.

Top: The Way Ahead, *1944. Coloured lithograph film poster by Abram Games.*

Above: *Major Harry Marshall Ford's entry in the College Roll of Honour.*

Postscript

The task of writing history is never complete, and our record of the Old Brightonians who died in the war and its aftermath is no exception. In compiling its roll of honour of the war dead, the College relied on information from family and other Old Brightonians. Some Old Boys will have had no close family; in other cases, families will not have contacted the College. A further complication is that in some instances no one back in Britain knew for sure whether a man had died or not for months or even years after the tragic event. Given this, inevitably some Old Brightonians who perished will be missing from this book. In a sense, they are the College's unknown warriors, and we commend them for their sacrifice. However, two Old Brightonians were discovered by the College after the main body of the book had been produced. Their entries are below.

Sub-Lieutenant Derek Barrington Jewell RNVR (Hampden House B 1932–34)

Killed in a naval battle on 1 March 1942, aged 23

Derek was born on 19 June 1918 to Sydney Jewell and his wife Dorothy (née Stone) of Westhampnett, Sussex. By the time he entered the College he was a local boy, living on Marine Parade, five minutes from the school. Derek's father gave his occupation at this time as engineer.

Jewell was killed during the Second Battle of the Java Sea, when his ship, the heavy cruiser HMS *Exeter*, was sunk by enemy surface ships. This opened the way for Japan's occupation of the Dutch East Indies.

The wreck of the *Exeter* was finally located in Indonesian waters 65 years after the battle, some 60 miles from the estimated sinking position, and she was declared an official war grave. However, when an expedition surveyed the site in 2016, it found that the wreck had been plundered for metal by illegal salvagers.

Above: *The cruiser HMS* Exeter, *1941.*

Sergeant Peter William Lewis Moore
(Hampden House A 1936–39)

Killed when his plane was shot down off the coast of Denmark on 27 August 1944, aged 22

Peter was born on 25 June 1922 to William Moore and his wife Eryl (née Lewis) of Hove, Sussex. At the time Peter entered the College his father was an actuary.

In 1944 Moore completed his RAF training, and was assigned to 57 Squadron at RAF East Kirkby in Lincolnshire, flying Lancaster bombers. To assist with the Allied advance, both before and after D-Day on 6 June 1944, he attacked a variety of targets in France, including coastal towns, a wireless station and a tank depot.

On the night of 26 August he took part in his first bombing mission against Germany, targeting Königsberg (now Kaliningrad in Russia), but his plane was shot down by a German Messerschmitt Bf 110 fighter near Tunø Island off the east coast of Denmark. The wreck was never found, and he is commemorated at the Runnymede Memorial to air force personnel with no known grave.

Peter was unlucky to fall victim to food poisoning the month before his death and miss a mission on the caves at Saint-Leu d'Esserent in France, which were used as storage depots for the deadly new V-1 bombs: his plane was shot down on that sortie, but the entire crew survived, with four of the six even evading capture.

Above: *Sergeant Peter Moore and his crew during training at RAF Syerston, May 1944. Peter is second from the left.*

Above: *Brighton College Roll of Honour, in date order. www.brightoncollegeremembers.com*

Acknowledgements

We would like to acknowledge everyone who helped produce this book, with particular thanks to:

James Harrison, Archivist Brighton College
Simon Smith, Brighton College Common Room 1973-2011
Nick Fraser, Deputy Headmaster (Innovation and Development)
Additionally from Brighton College:
  Abigail Wharne, Former Archivist
  Joe Skeaping, Former Head of History
  Oliver Thicknesse, Classics master
  Charlotte Thackray, Volunteer Researcher
  Ornella Hulbert, Volunteer Researcher
  Ted Batt, Hampden 1939–44
  Alice Fowler, Proofreader
Anita Baker
Battle of Britain London Monument
Brighton & Hove City Council
Commonwealth War Graves Commission
David McHugh, Photographer
Dulwich College
H.M.S. Hood Association
Hornchurch Aerodrome Historical Society
Imperial War Museum
The National Archives
The National Library of Singapore
The National Portrait Gallery
Paradata
The Regency Society and The James Gray Collection
Royal Pavilion and Museums Brighton and Hove
Scottish National War Museum
Relatives of the fallen:
  Oscar Ackerman
  Hugh Acworth
  Christopher Chave
  Lesley Margaret Cherry
  Josephine Stewart Ferguson
  Alfred Fleming
  Eleanor Good
  James Godfrey Higham
  Jennifer Higham

Nicholas Humpherson
Juliet Kensington
William Lonsdale
Sir Christopher Mallaby, GCMG, GCVO
Max Manning
Iain McIver
Philip Nunn
The Sulman family

With thanks to our 4th Form pupils and their families 2017–18

Rachael ABERGEL Fenwick
Billy ALBU Leconfield
Herbie ARMSTRONG Head's
Kate BALDOCK Chichester
William BANKS Abraham
Tilly BERTELSEN Williams
Bede BLABER School House
Oliver BLOMFIELD Leconfield
Maddy BRAITHWAITE Williams
Finley BRAUND Ryle
Cooper BROWN Aldrich
Noah BRYANT Leconfield
Daniel BURKE Durnford
Luna CABRERA HULBERT Williams
James CARMICHAEL Leconfield
Lara CLAYSON Williams
Paul Kaan COFFIN School House
Jake CRANE Aldrich
Joe CRONJE Ryle
Joshua DAVIDSON School House
Rohan DIWAKAR Hampden
Max DOMBROWE Durnford
Jamie EVANS Aldrich
Isabelle FARLAM Seldon
Maria FERRERO Williams
Max FURTH School House
Jack GARDNER Hampden
Isaac GLASSBROOK Abraham
Jack GRAY Head's
Eren GURYEL Leconfield
Alex HARRISON Durnford
Tom HELPS Aldrich
Alex HODGSON Seldon
Samuel HORSBRUGH Hampden
Sophie HYDE Seldon
Andrew JACKSON Leconfield
Ruby JERGES Chichester
Abby LAMBERT Seldon

Defne AKYILDIZ Chichester
James ARMITAGE School House
Jamie ASQUITH Leconfield
Tom BALKWILL-SIMMONS Hampden
Aurora BARRERA JAMES Seldon
Henry BISHOP Ryle
Sam BLATCHFORD Ryle
Sophie BRADLEY Seldon
Laura BRAUN New House
Dan BREWER Hampden
Harry BROWNE Hampden
Ben BURCHELL Hampden
Isaac BUTLER-KING Durnford
Aran CAMPBELL Aldrich
Suzette CHEN Seldon
Max CODDINGTON Abraham
Zac COXEN Head's
Max CRAWFORD-COLLINS Head's
Pun DANCHAIVICHIT School House
Jad DBOUK Abraham
Ella DOMANSKA Fenwick
Eva ELLICOCK Chichester
Matilda EVANS Chichester
Grace FARROW-MOORE New House
Leif FINDLAY Leconfield
Adriana GARCIA ALUMBREROS Williams
Savannah GEMMELL Fenwick
Ben GOOLEY Head's
Owen GRIFFIN-BALLARD Ryle
Leo HARRIS Ryle
Blossom HARRISON-HALES New House
Alexandra HIRONS Williams
Guy HONEY Aldrich
Elodie HYDE Chichester
Bill IRELAND-MYATT Ryle
Ravi JADAV Hampden
Jake KUMP Aldrich
Oscar LANZALACO School House

Milo LARCOMBE Leconfield
Tom LAWRENCE Aldrich
Camden LEYHANE Head's
Yuzhe LIN Head's
Arthur LOGAN Ryle
Sophie MALE New House
Sam MASTERS Head's
Toby McCALL Leconfield
Emie McGEOUGH Seldon
Barney MILLS Head's
Simran MOGER Fenwick
Catherine MORLEY New House
Zak NOWSHADI Durnford
Scott OKONKWO Leconfield
Alex OWEN Aldrich
Evie PAGE Seldon
Rishil PATEL School House
Matias PAZ LINARES School House
Scarlett PHILLIPS Seldon
Oliver POINTEAU Abraham
Tanya PRAKASH Williams
Davey PROTHERO Hampden
Yardan RAJAP Durnford
Seth RICKARD Leconfield
James RING Leconfield
Tarun ROHILLA Aldrich
Theo ROSS Aldrich
Sophie SABIN New House
Johnny SALIB Aldrich
Luca SHEARER Abraham
Ben SMITH Durnford
Lily SMITH Fenwick
Tom SMITH Durnford
Jamie SPIERS Durnford
George STEWART Abraham
George SWALLOW Abraham
Don TAN Abraham
Winston TANG School House
Stephen TAYLOR Aldrich
Athena THOMAS New House
Roxy TOYNE Chichester
Holly TURNBULL Chichester
Rosie WADE Fenwick
Ella WARD Williams
Phoebe WHEELER New House
Layla WILKINSON Fenwick
Noah WILMAN Head's
Tom WRIGHT Ryle

Lucy LAW Williams
Seung-Won LEE Hampden
Fenn LILLEY Durnford
Honor LINDSAY New House
Ross MACKENZIE Durnford
Miles MAO Hampden
Isabella MASTRIFORTE Chichester
Rachael McEVOY Chichester
Lucy MERMAGEN New House
Olivia MINUCCI Fenwick
Finn MOLL School
Minnie NOAR Seldon
Milo O'DONAHUE School House
Dillon OLORENSHAW Hampden
Tom PADLEY Abraham
Amber PATEL Chichester
Shiven PATEL Ryle
Shaun PEXTON Ryle
Pietro PIGNATTI MORANO CAMPORI School House
Azaria POWER Seldon
Detty PRIOR Williams
Sienna PUDNEY Fenwick
Gus REDDING Aldrich
Harrison RIGBY Durnford
Freddie ROBERTS Leconfield
Connor ROOK Leconfield
Ollie RYDER Durnford
Zoe SAKS Williams
Anvi SANATHI Williams
Sabina SIMPSON Seldon
Lauryn SMITH New House
Melissa SMITH New House
Florence SOLE Williams
Lottie SPINK Seldon
Branislav STOJANOVSKI Hampden
Oliver TAITE JUPP Ryle
Eric TANG Head's
Eve TAYLOR Chichester
Eloise TEMPLAR EARL Chichester
Muraco TO New House
Edward TREVILLION Ryle
Harsha VITTA Durnford
Por WAIWITLIKHIT Head's
Timothy WERGAN Head's
Bonnie WHITE Chichester
Dylan WILLIAMS Aldrich
Felix WINSTANLEY Hampden
Rueben YU Abraham

Copyright Information

For images not in the public domain, copyright is held by Brighton College, except those listed below:

Title	Page No.	Copyright
Sunday Express front page, 3 September 1939	10	Alamy
Military Cross	13	Ministry of Defence
The burnt-out car of the late Brigadier Mallaby	14	Imperial War Museum (SE 5724)
Alfred Fleming	15	Alfred Fleming (son)
John Pelham Acworth dressed as a beggar	16	Hugh Acworth
Poster for the film *The Great Escape*	19	Alamy
HMS *Royal Oak*, 1937	27	Imperial War Museum (FL 12252)
Grave of Flying Officer Peter Edward Torkington-Leech, Honington (All Saints) Churchyard, Suffolk	27	The War Graves Photographic Project
Anson aircraft ready to take off	29	Imperial War Museum (HU 129267)
Portrait of Neville Chamberlain	33	National Portrait Gallery, London (NPG 4279)
British Soldiers wading out to a waiting destroyer off Dunkirk	34	Imperial War Museum (HU 41240)
Painting *Embarkation of Wounded, May 1940*, by Edward Bawden	34	Imperial War Museum (Art.IWM ART LD 6337)
Still from the 2007 film *Atonement*	35	Alamy
Painting *The Little Ships at Dunkirk*, by Norman Wilkinson	35	Imperial War Museum (Art.IWM ART LD 6007)
Officers of 'B' Flight 65 Squadron, including Desmond Cooke	37	Hornchurch Aerodrome Historical Society
Poster for *The Ghost Comes Home*	40	Alamy
Saloon bar of 'The Cricketers' pub in Brighton during 1944	42	Imperial War Museum (D 22509)
Car passes a sandbagged barricade on the A23 road near Brighton, 1940	42	Imperial War Museum (H 1946)
Brighton beach, packed with holiday makers during the spring of 1940	42	Brighton and Hove City Council
Brighton Beach in 1940 with anti-invasion measures	42	Royal Pavilion and Museums, Brighton & Hove
Map showing where bombs landed in Brighton and Hove, 1944	43	Royal Pavilion and Museums, Brighton & Hove
Aftermath from a bombing in Brighton	43	Andy Garth, of Brighton Hove and Stuff
Bristol Beaufort aircraft in flight	44	Imperial War Museum (TR 31)
Men of the Leicestershire Regiment at Tobruk	46	Imperial War Museum (E 6436)
Halfaya Sollum War Cemetery, Egypt	47	Commonwealth War Graves Commission
Archibald Dooley Brankston's book, *Early Ming Wares of Chingtechen*	54	Vetch and Lee LTD, London
Air Warden Poster	58	Imperial War Museum (Art.IWM PST 13880)

Title	Page No.	Copyright
HMS *Express*	60	Imperial War Museum (A 534)
HMS *Avenger*	60	Imperial War Museum (FL 1268)
HMS *Hood* with the crew paraded	60	Imperial War Museum (HU 76083)
HMS *Glengyle*	61	Imperial War Museum (FL 22266)
HMS *Colsay*	61	Imperial War Museum (FL 8287)
HMS *Electra*	61	Imperial War Museum (FL 24524)
John Humpherson in the cockpit	62	Nick Humpherson
DFC Medal	62	Ministry of Defence
Daylight raid on the docks at Rotterdam by Bristol Blenheims	64	Imperial War Museum (C 1948)
Sir Edmund Keith Nuttall	68	National Portrait Gallery, London (NPG x123367)
Bofors anti-aircraft gun being dug in	69	Imperial War Museum (E 18689)
Vickers Wellington bombers over the Western Desert	70	Imperial War Museum (ME(RAF) 3699)
Hurricane fighter over England	70	Imperial War Museum (MH 3186)
Blenheim bomber over the North Sea	70	Imperial War Museum (MH 140)
Hampden bomber in flight above clouds	70	Imperial War Museum (COL 182)
Hawker Hart bomber	70	Imperial War Museum (MH 31)
Armourers poised to load a Short Stirling with bombs	71	Imperial War Museum (CH 5135)
Avro Lancaster bombers	71	Imperial War Museum (TR 197)
Martin Baltimore bomber	71	Imperial War Museum (CNA 2584)
Boston III light bomber and reconnaissance aircraft	71	Imperial War Museum (CM 2084)
Handley Page Halifax bomber	71	Imperial War Museum (HU 92965)
Lockheed Hudson bomber and reconnaissance aircraft	71	Imperial War Museum (COL 183)
Francis Hugh Twycross-Raines	72	Dulwich College (Image reproduced with kind permission of the Governors of Dulwich College)
HMS *Barnham* explosion	72	Imperial War Museum ((MOI) FLM 1984)
Newly arrived British troops at Singapore give the 'thumbs up'	77	Imperial War Museum (FE 312)
HMS *Prince of Wales* and *Repulse* after being hit by Japanese torpedoes	80	Imperial War Museum (HU 2762)
Art depicting prisoners of war carrying a large log across the River Kwai in Thailand	80	Imperial War Museum (Art.IWM ART LD 6035)
Troops loading a jeep into a Douglas Dakota Mark III of No. 194 Squadron RAF	80	Imperial War Museum (CF 145)
Poster for the 1957 film *The Bridge on the River Kwai*	81	Alamy
Sketch depicting boot repairing by POWs	81	Imperial War Museum (HU 3071)
Lieutenant-General Arthur Percival and his party carrying the Union Jack on their way to surrender Singapore to the Japanese	81	Imperial War Museum (HU 2781)
Group photograph of 'Miss Diana Shelley's friends', 1931	83	National Library of Singapore
John Pelham Acworth's marriage to Jean Craig Wallace	84	Hugh Acworth

Title	Page No.	Copyright
5.5-inch gun of the 178th Medium Regiment in action	121	Imperial War Museum (NA 21006)
Soldiers resting by the roadside, by Edward Jeffrey Irving, 1943	121	Imperial War Museum (Art.IWM ART LD 3457)
Flushing (Vlissingen) Northern Cemetery	122	Commonwealth War Graves Commission
French's Acting Edition of *Shivering Shocks*, by Clemence Dane	125	Samuel French Limited, London (1923)
Percy Godfrey Openshaw	129	Jennifer Higham
Port side of HMS *Penelope*, April 1942	129	Imperial War Museum (A 8603)
Caterpillar Club membership card	131	Oscar Ackerman
Prisoner of war wanted poster	133	Imperial War Museum (HU 21187)
Art depicting wounded British soldiers	136	Imperial War Museum (Art.IWM ART LD 4280)
Art depicting the landing in Normandy	136	Imperial War Museum (Art.IWM ART LD 5816)
Art depicting General Montgomery	137	Private collection; on loan to the National Portrait Gallery, London (NPG L165)
Art depicting British soldiers and American Navy ratings sitting on a landing craft	137	Imperial War Museum (Art.IWM ART LD 4087)
King George VI inspecting the 6th Airborne Division, 16 March 1944	138	Imperial War Museum (H 36704)
John Anthony Colson Fitch	149	Paradata
Painting of 51st Highland Division planning of El Alamein	151	Scottish National War Museum (M.2018.20)
John Henry Lloyd Sulman, with his brother Hugh	153	Sarah Dean
Poster for the 1952 film, *The Snows of Kilimanjaro*	154	Alamy
Peter Wyatt-Smith	158	Battle of Britain London Monument
Kenneth David Gordon Phillips	158	Josephine Stewart Ferguson
Taukkyan War Cemetery, Myanmar	159	Commonwealth War Graves Commission
Mosquito aircraft over England	159	Imperial War Museum (CH 12415)
Flying Officer Raymond Julius Guy Manning	160	Max Manning
Singapore Memorial	163	Commonwealth War Graves Commission
Poster for *The Way Ahead* film	167	National Army Museum (NAM. 2013-07-2-1) © Estate of Abram Games
HMS *Exeter*	168	Imperial War Museum (A 3553)
Sergeant Peter Moore and his crew during training at RAF Syerston, May 1944	169	Michael Davies
John Pelham Acworth in military attire	171	Hugh Acworth
Commonwealth forces poster from the Second World War	181	Imperial War Museum (Art.IWM PST 3158)

TOGETHER

Above: *Together. Commonwealth forces poster from the Second World War. Seven Old Brightonians from Commonwealth countries were among the fallen (five from Australia, one from New Zealand and one from Canada), as well as Old Brightonians from Argentina, Peru, Russia, the Netherlands and Germany. Nine Old Brightonians fought in the Indian colonial forces, while one fought in the Malayan forces.*

Index

References to images are in *italics*.